I0483405

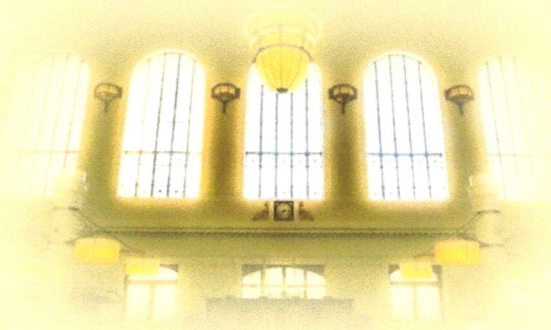

– Zephyr –
a soft, gentle breeze

Riding a Zephyr into the Past

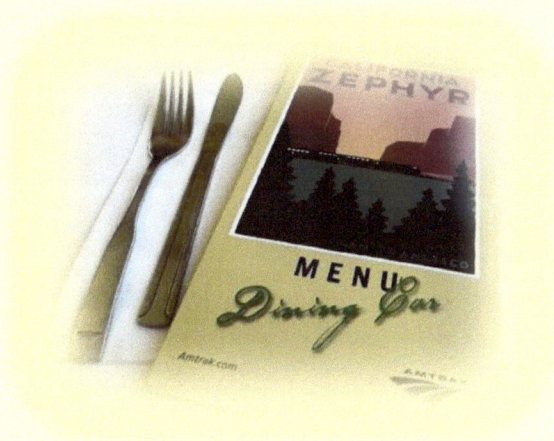

Images from Atwood

Riding a Zephyr into the Past
Images from Atwood

Copyright 2016, Echo Hill Arts Press, LLC
All rights reserved, including the right to reproduce any part of this book.
ISBN: 978-0-9975819-3-5
Colorado Springs, CO, USA

ECHO HILL ARTS PRESS

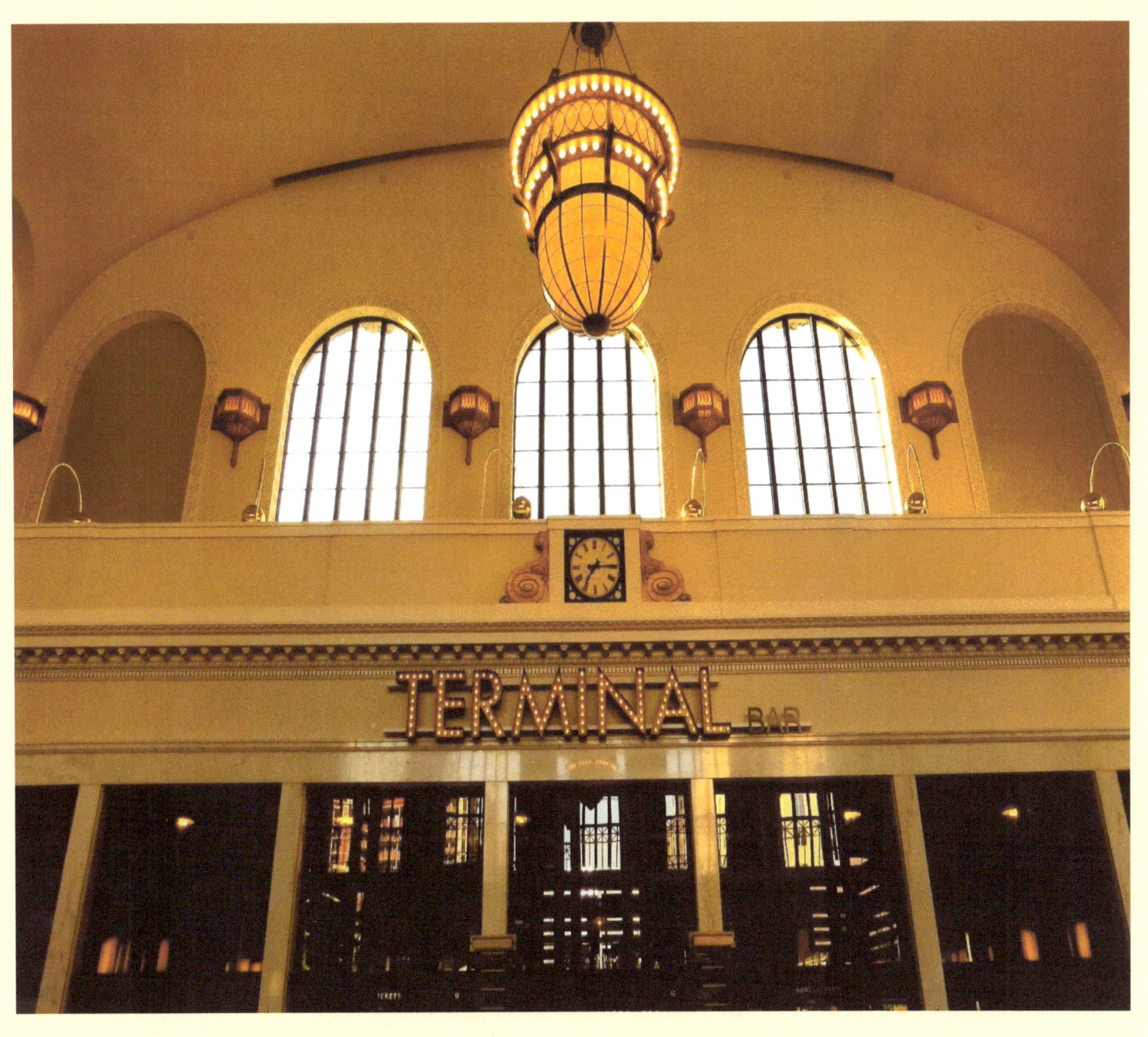

Starting at Denver's Union Station –

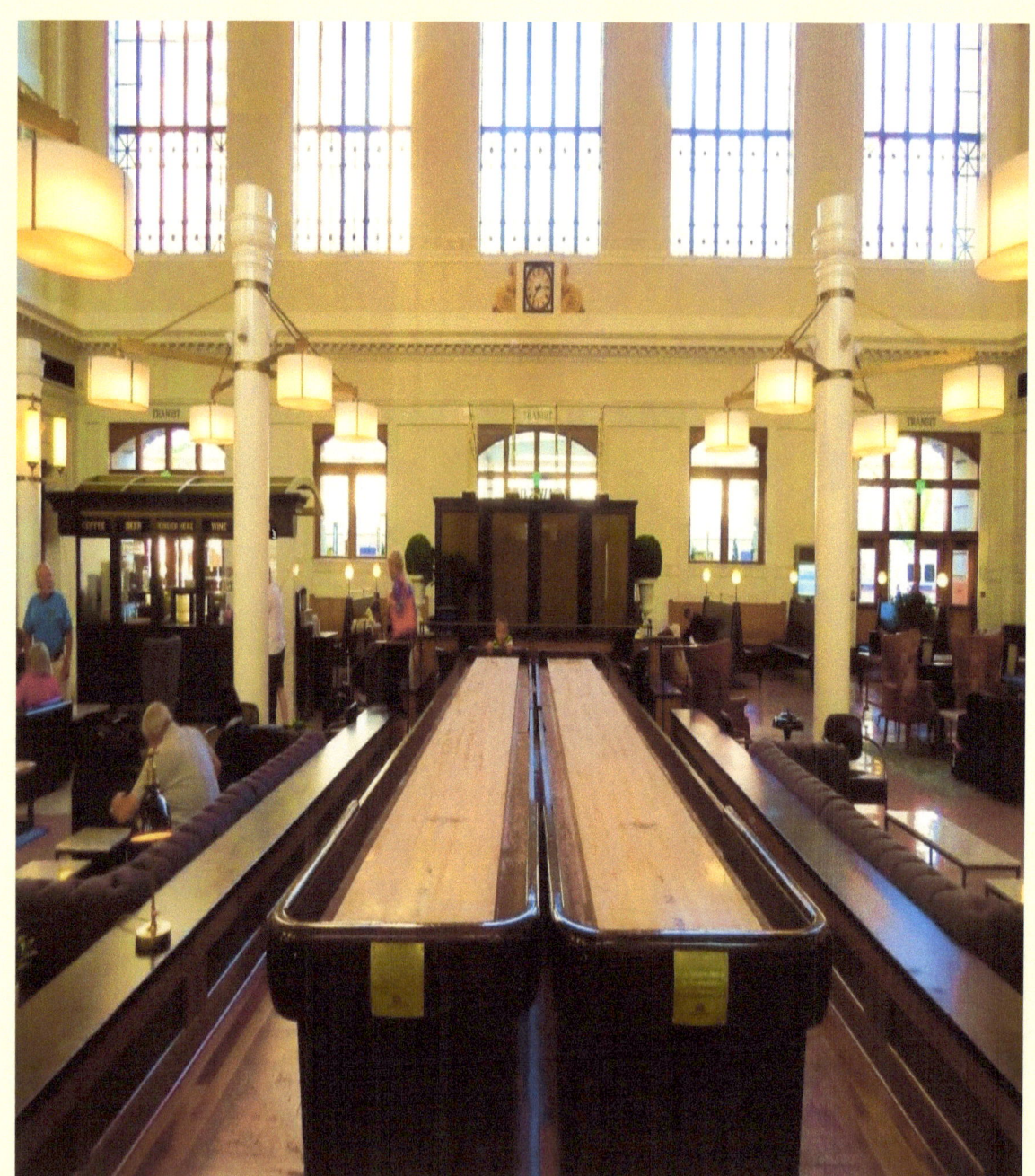

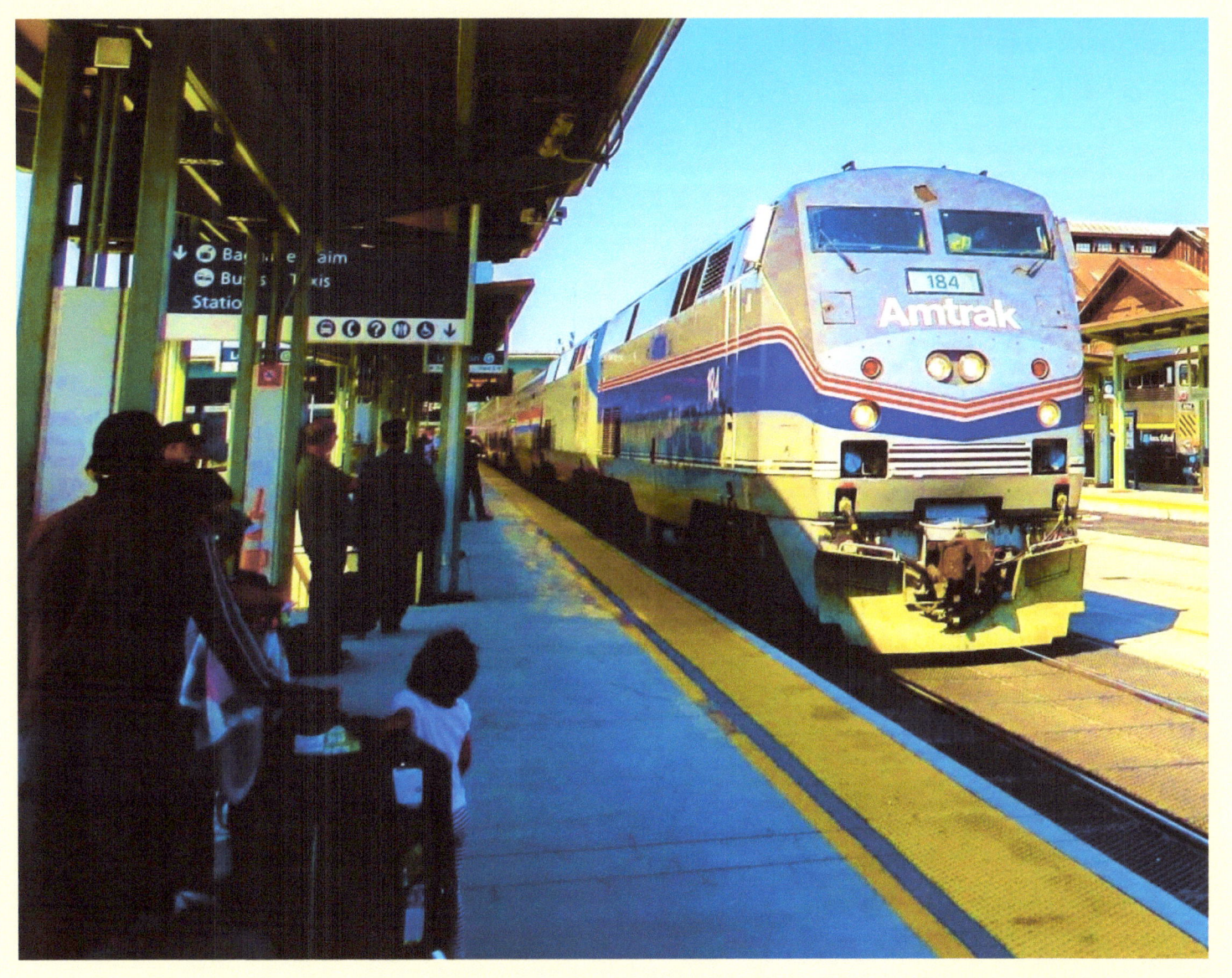

*Several voyagers wait to board
a California Zephyr heading west –
Wishing to leave the intensity of their city –*

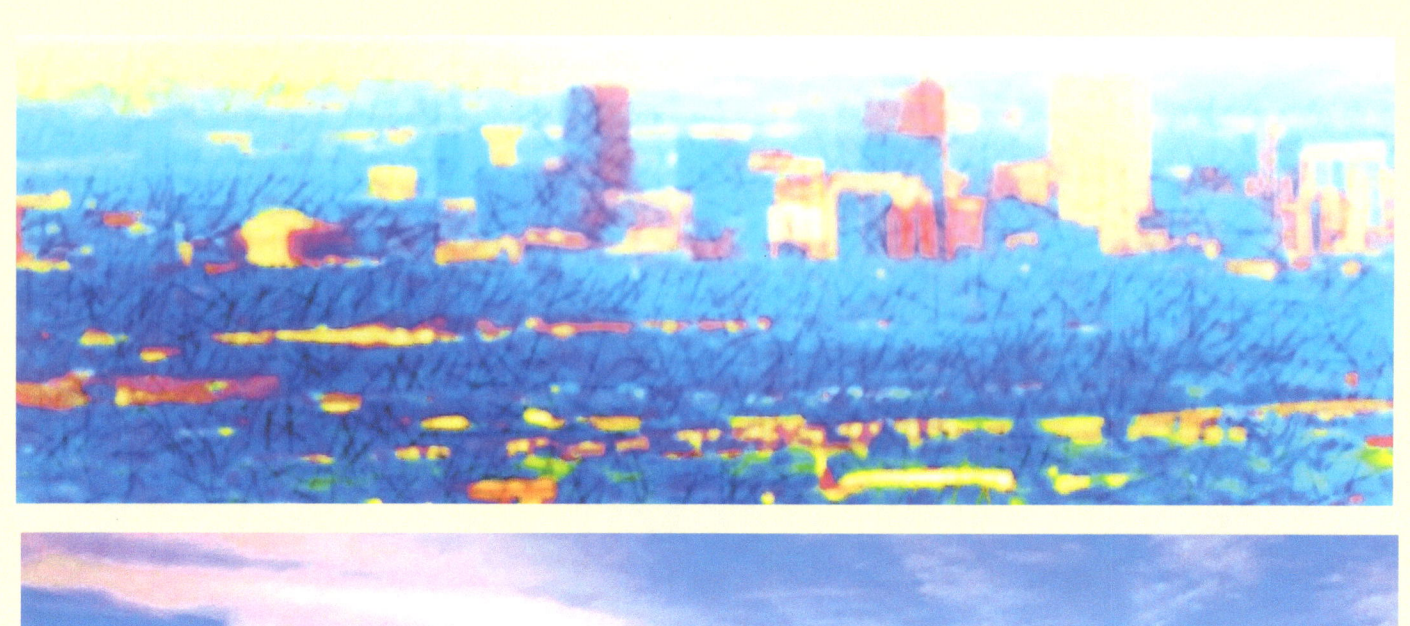

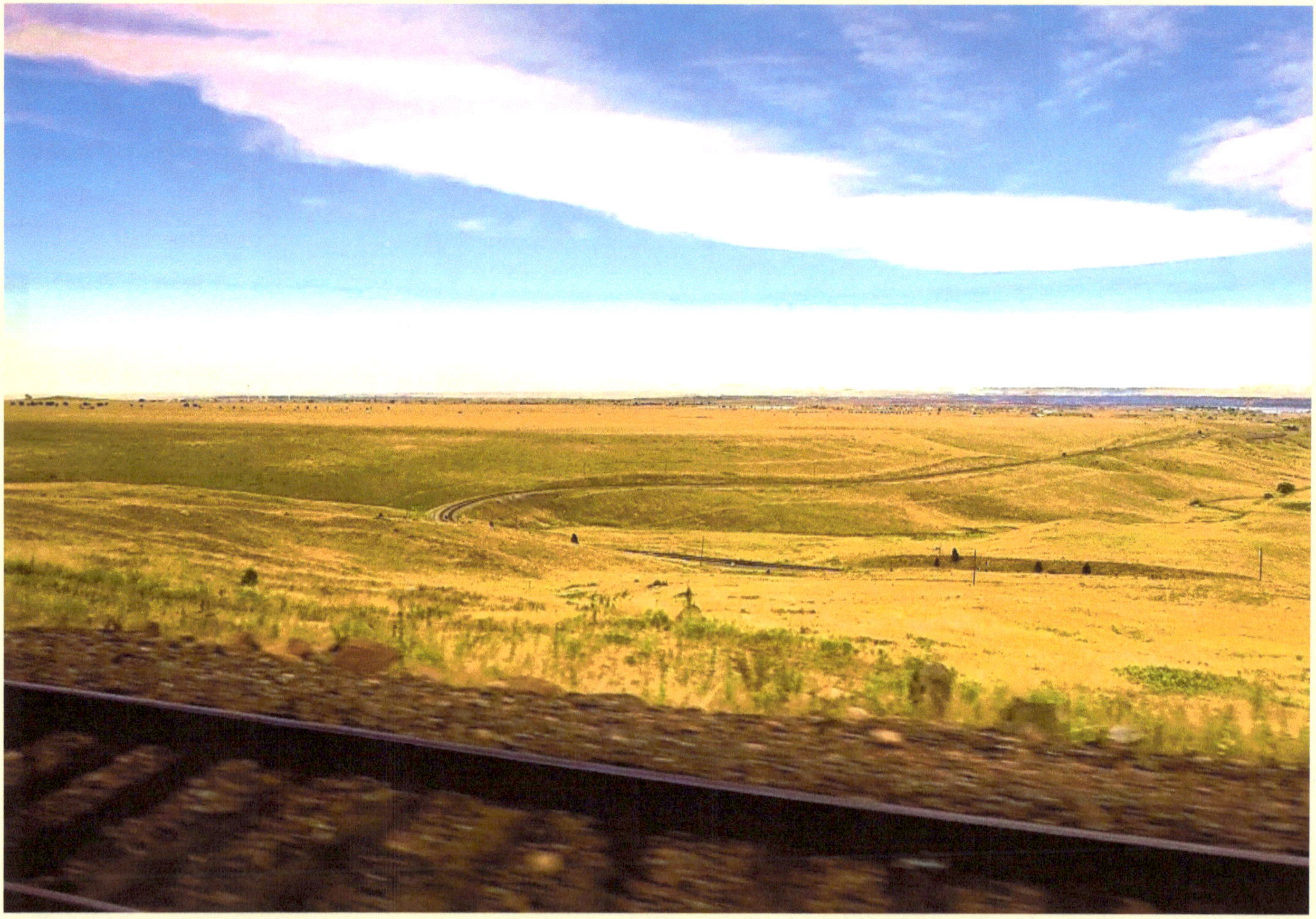

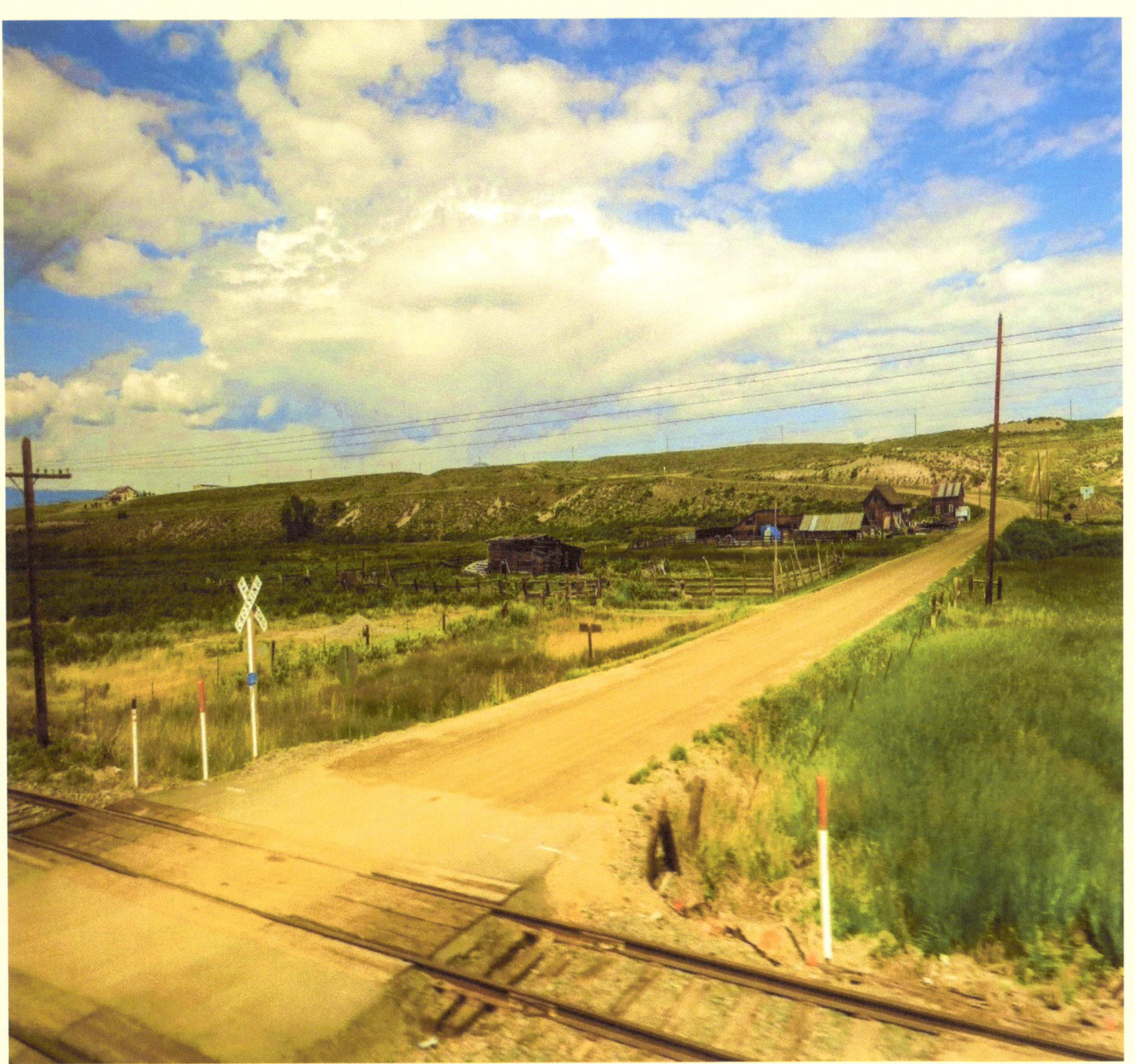

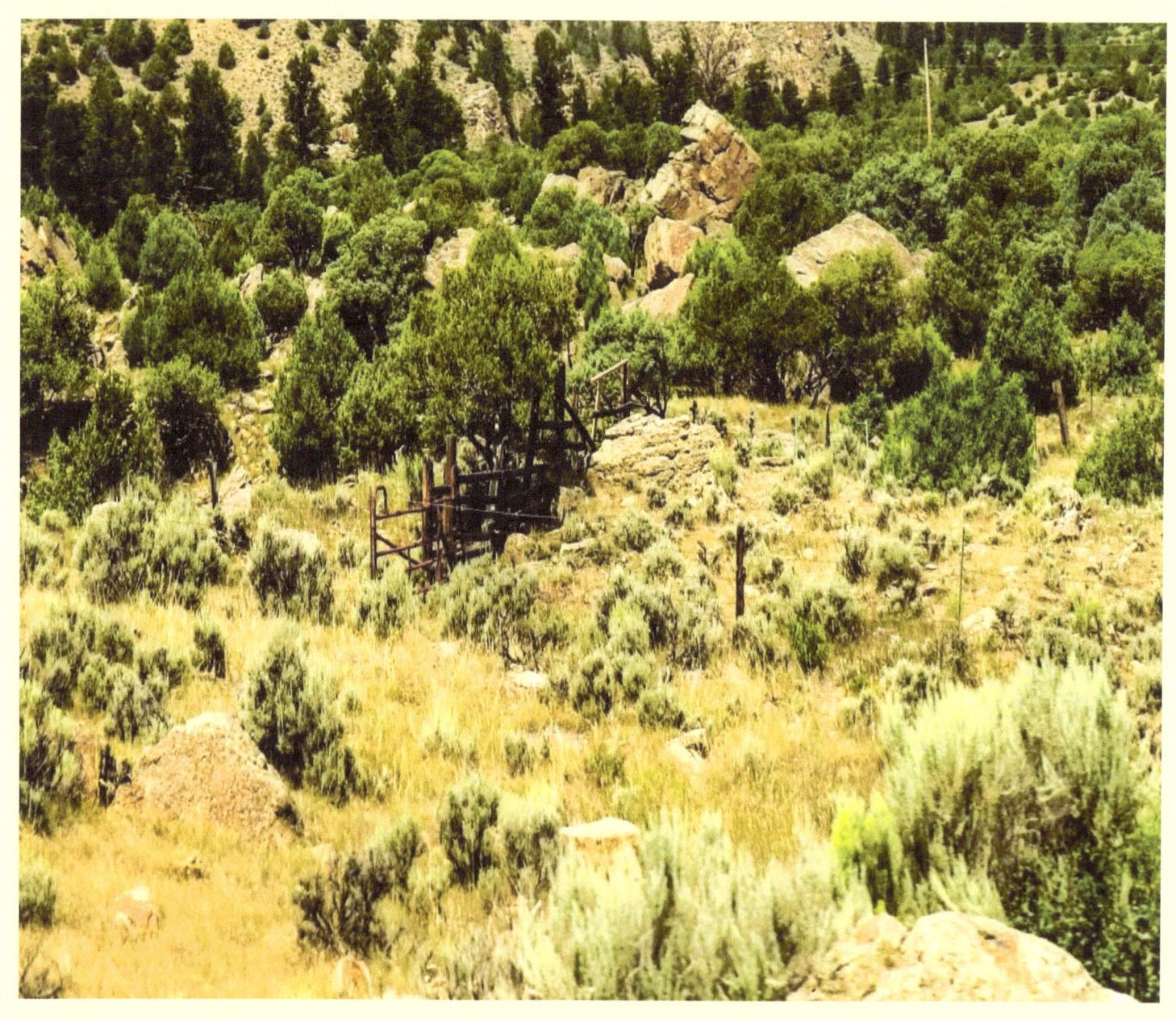

by climbing high into the Rockies –

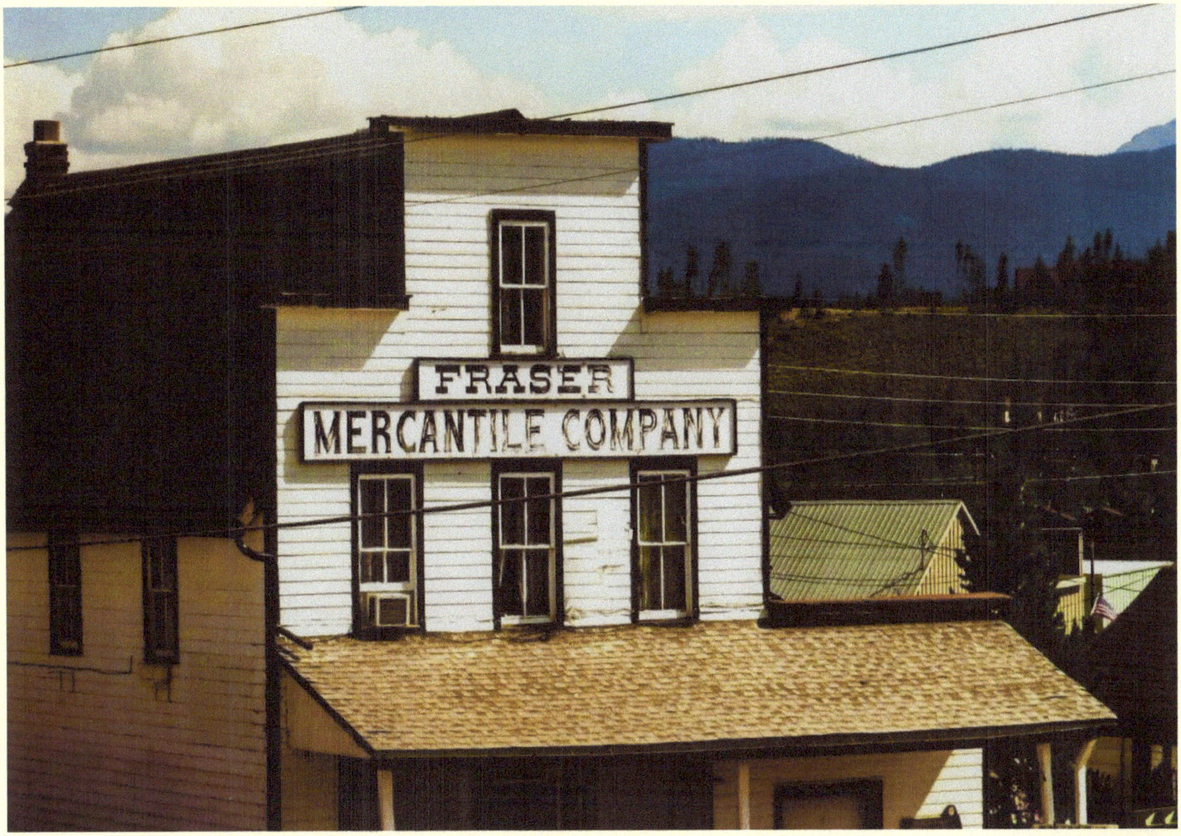

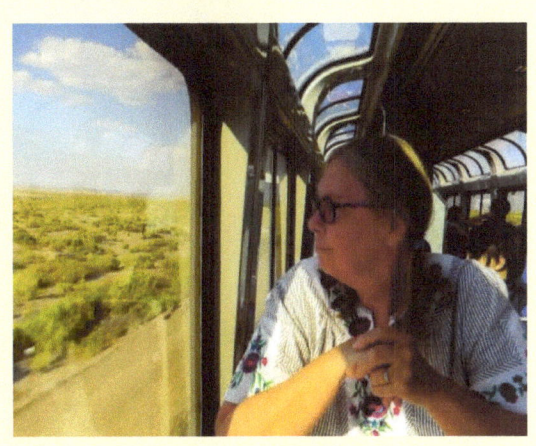

To be whisked away, as on a breeze,

West ward into an earlier time –

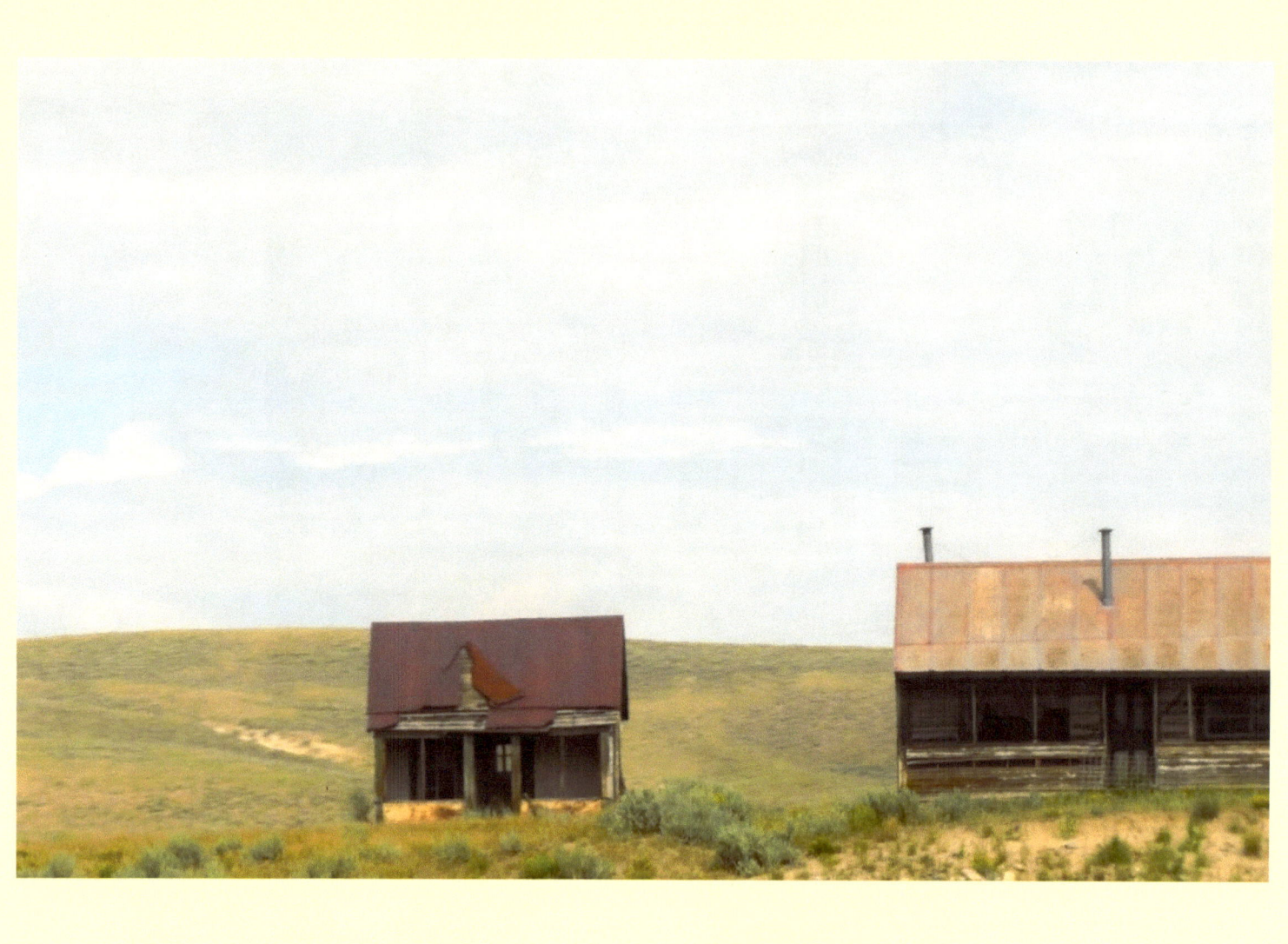

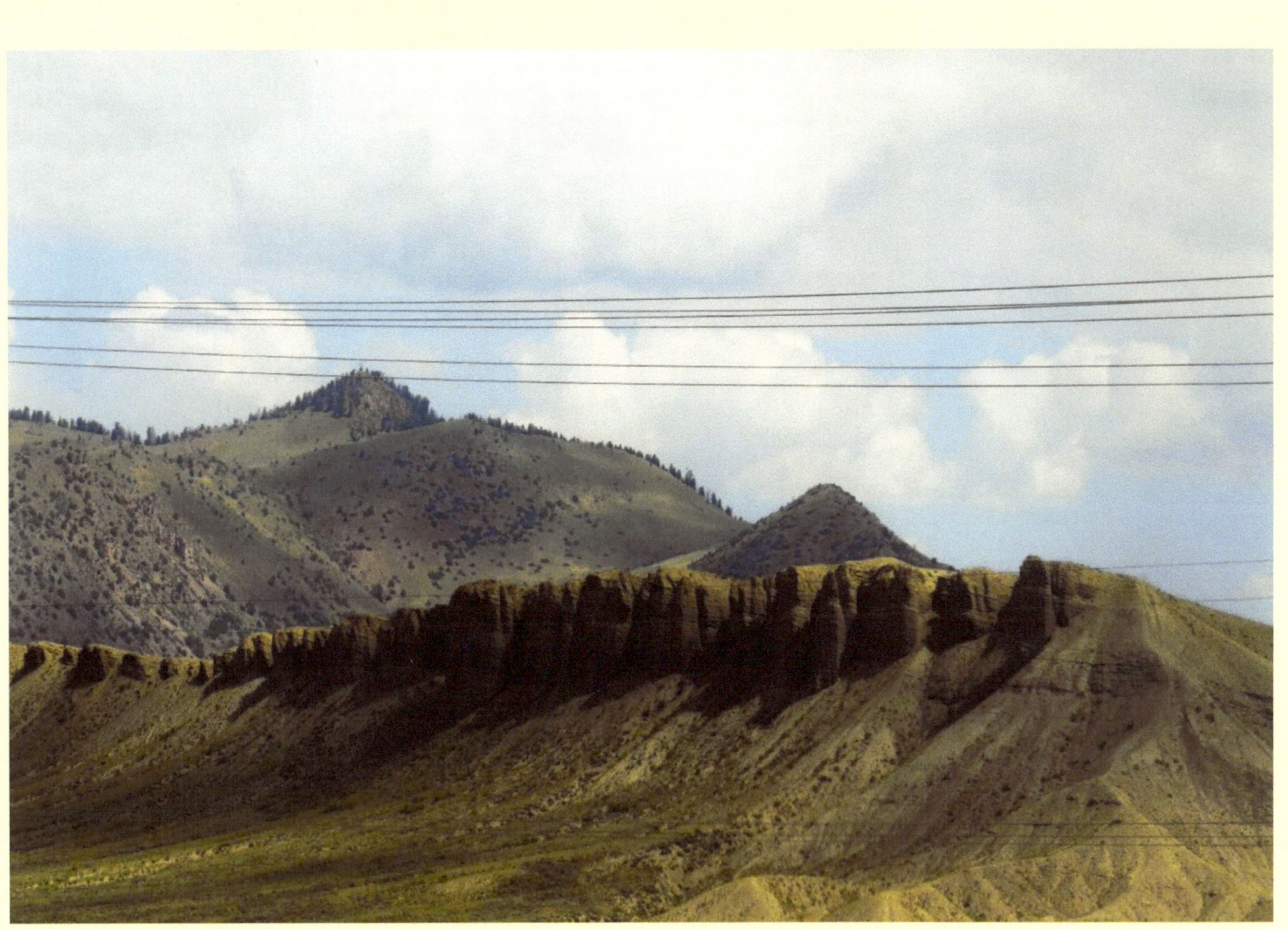

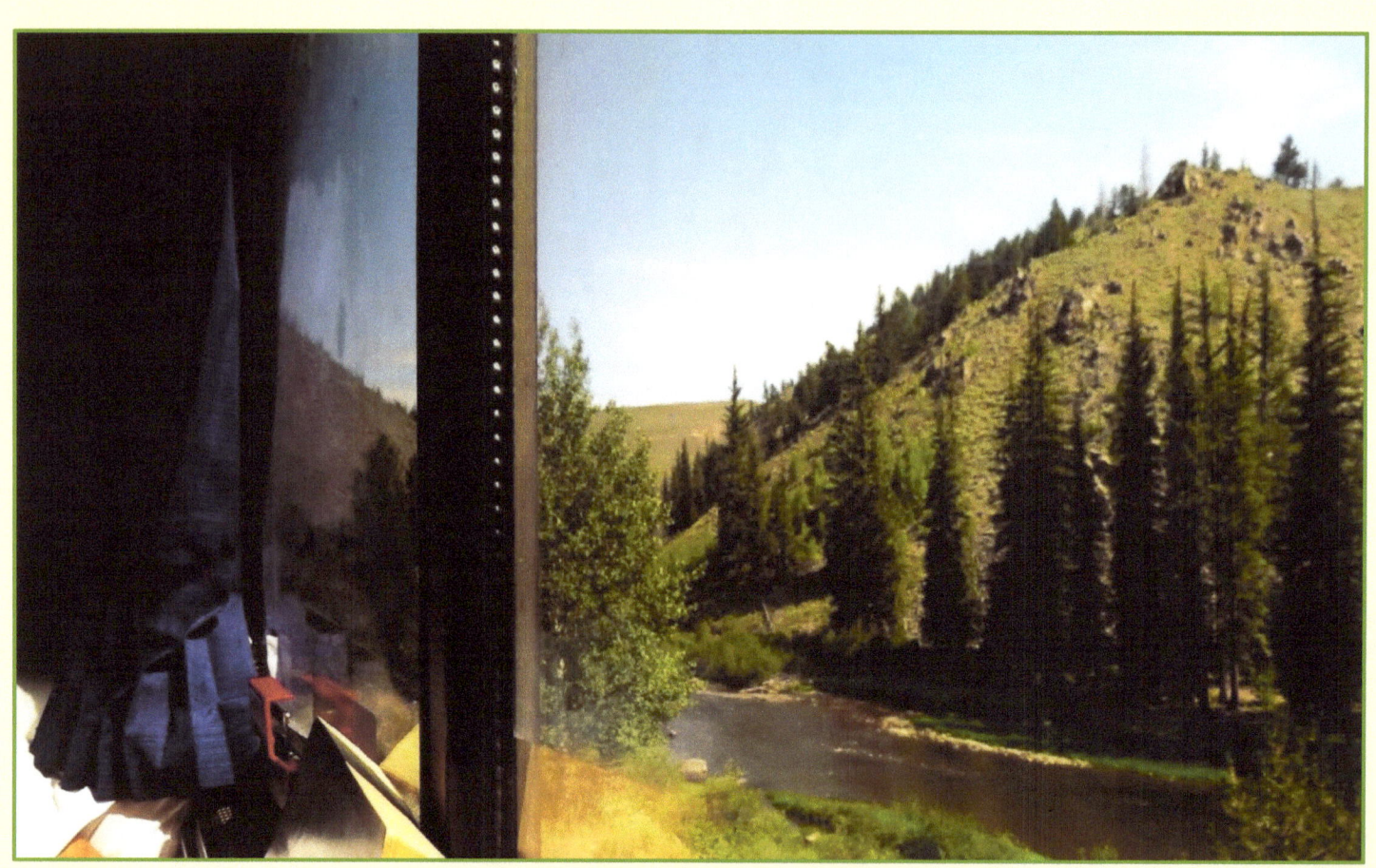

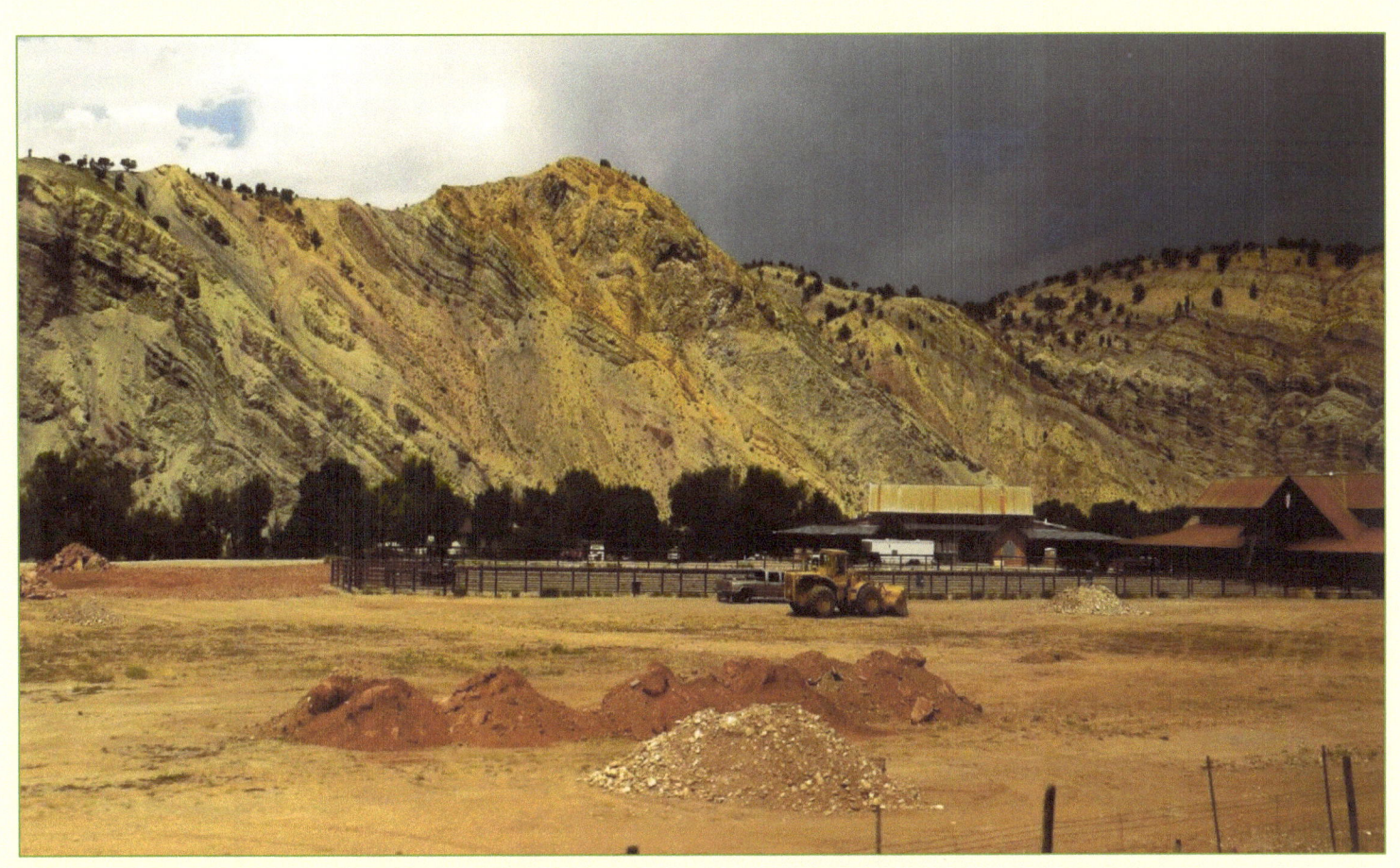

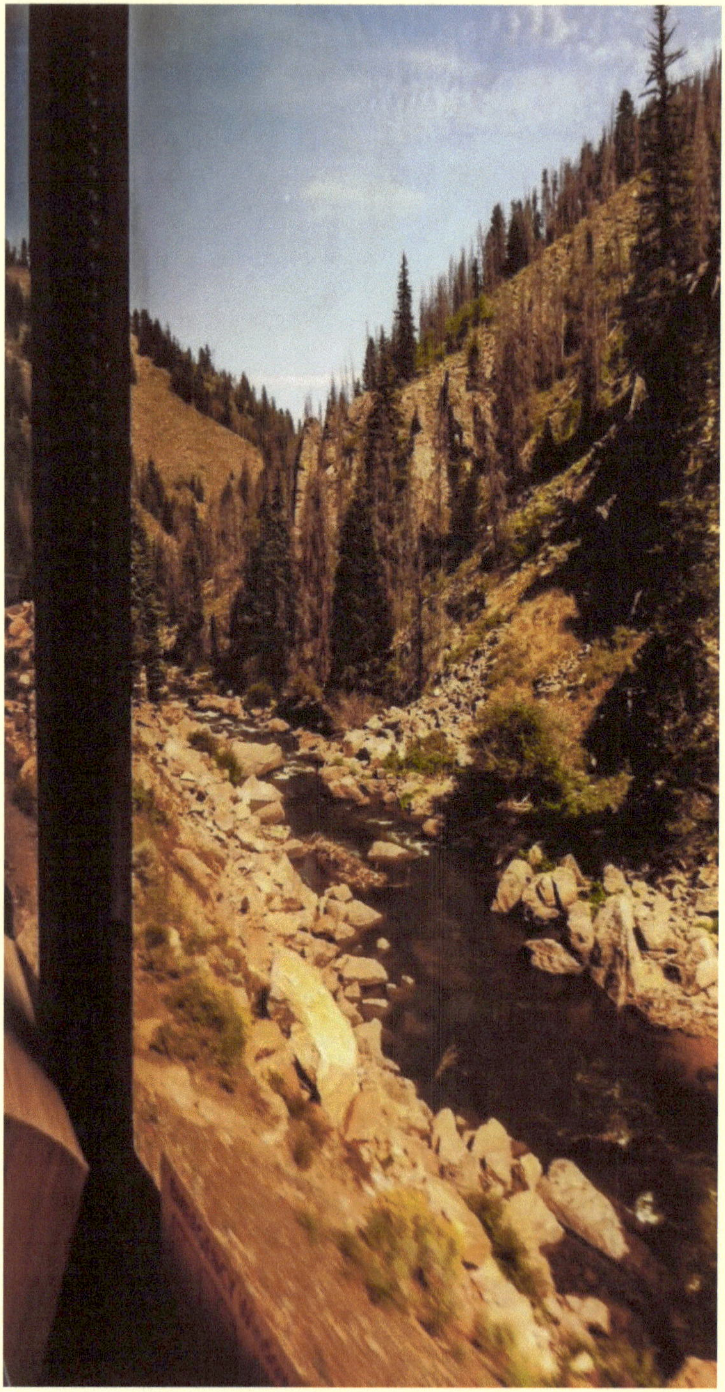
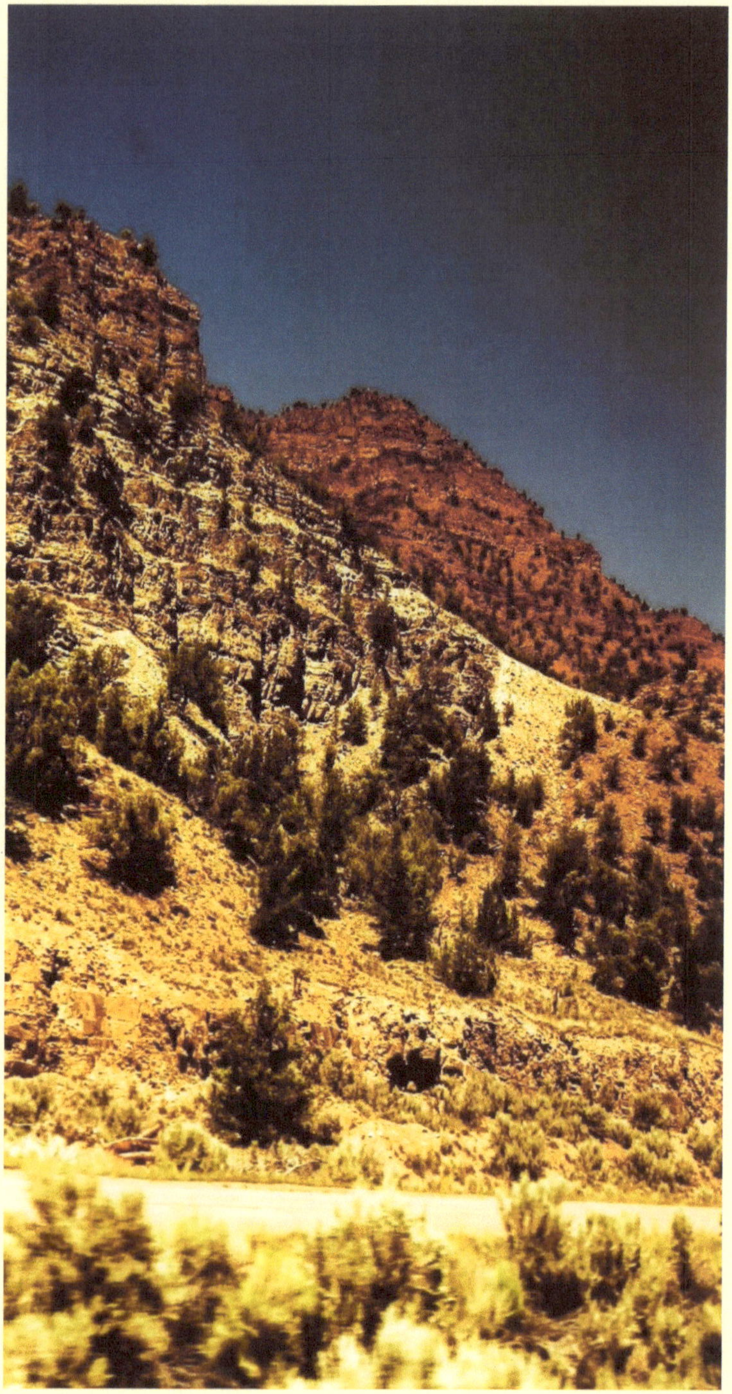

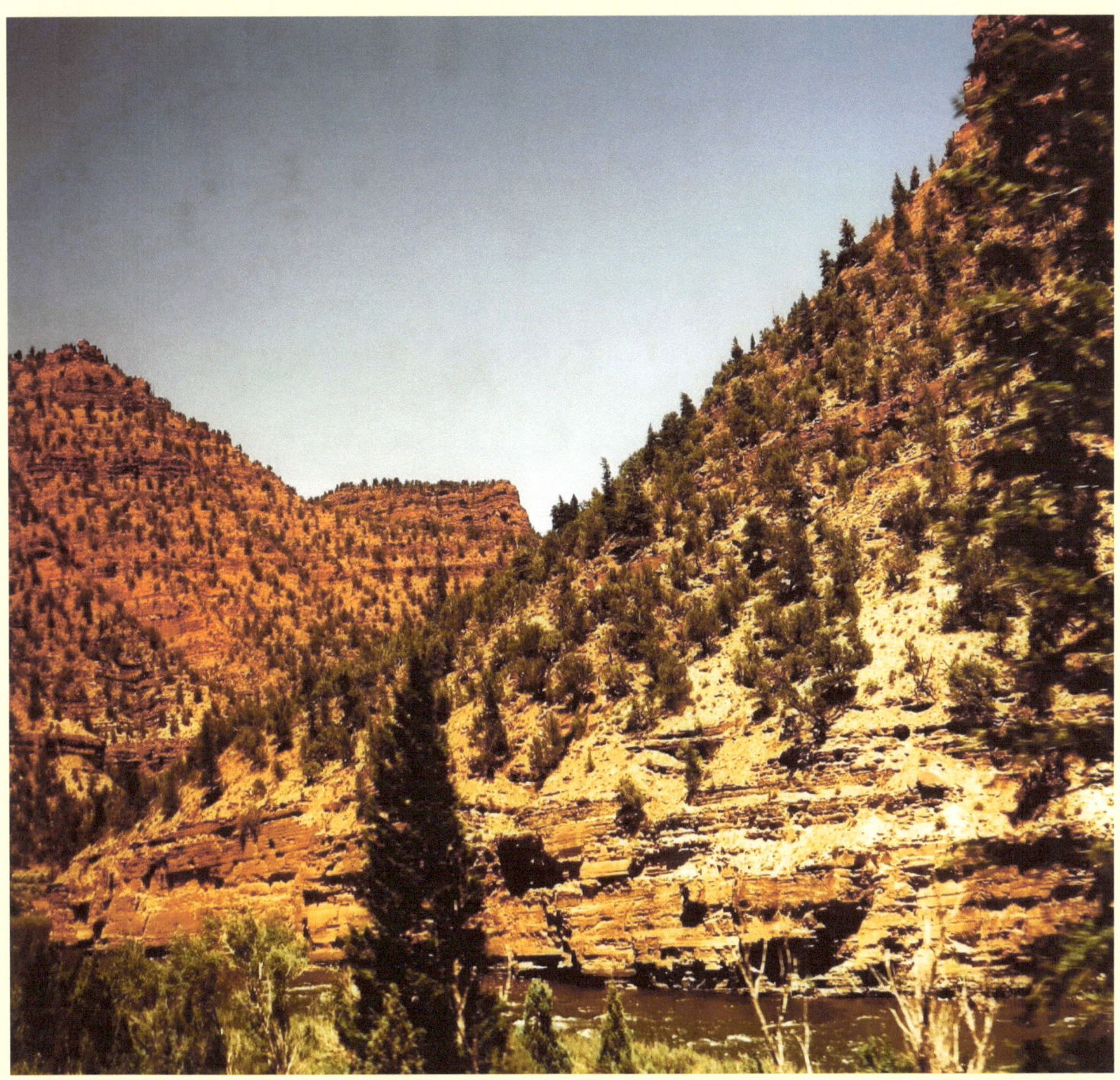

Undulating along red walls of gorges,
and rolling through green valleys worn flat

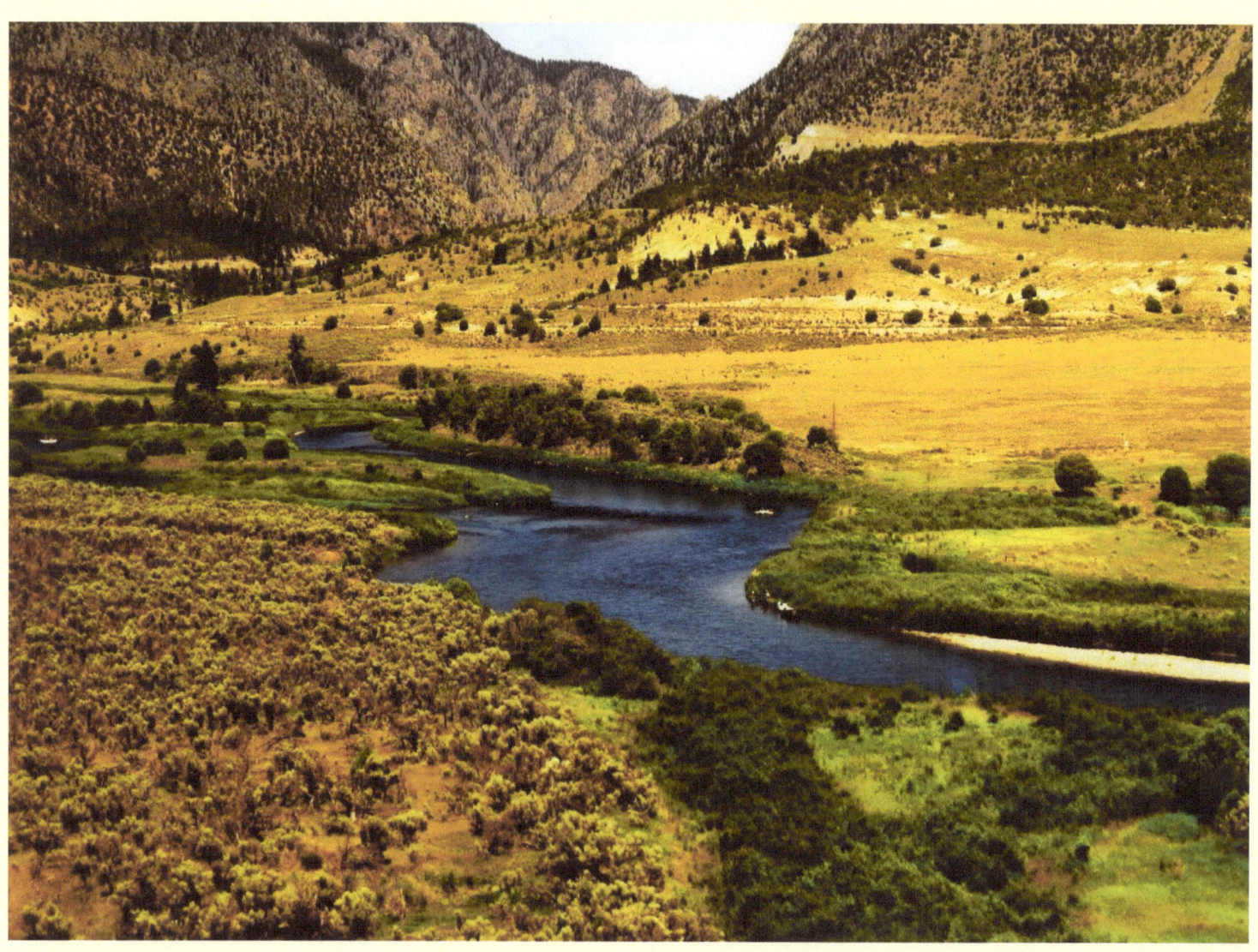

by waters shed eastward along the ridge of great separation –

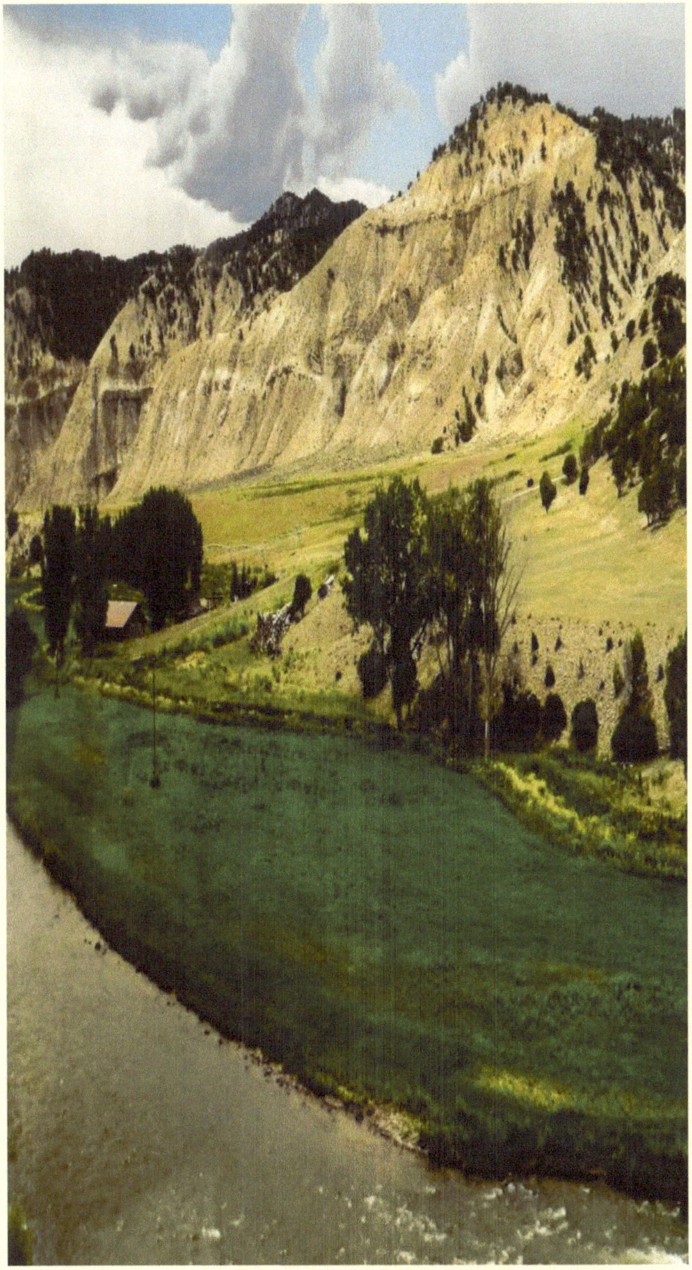

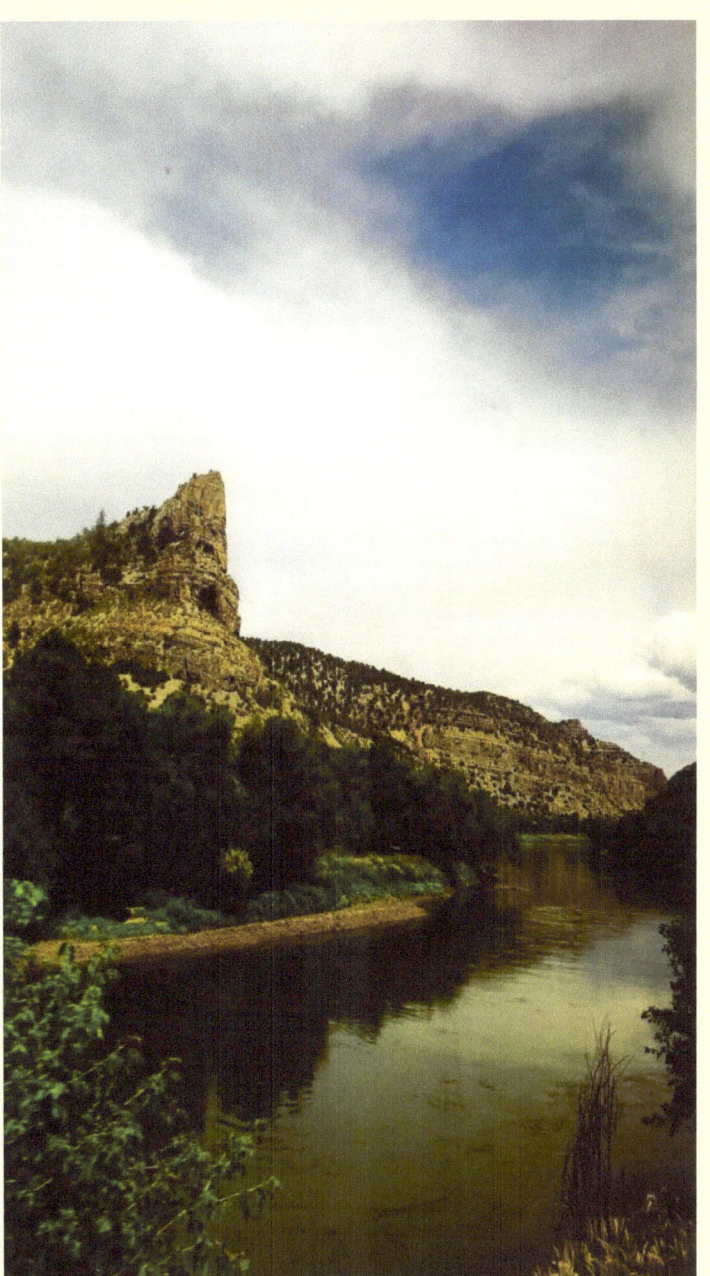

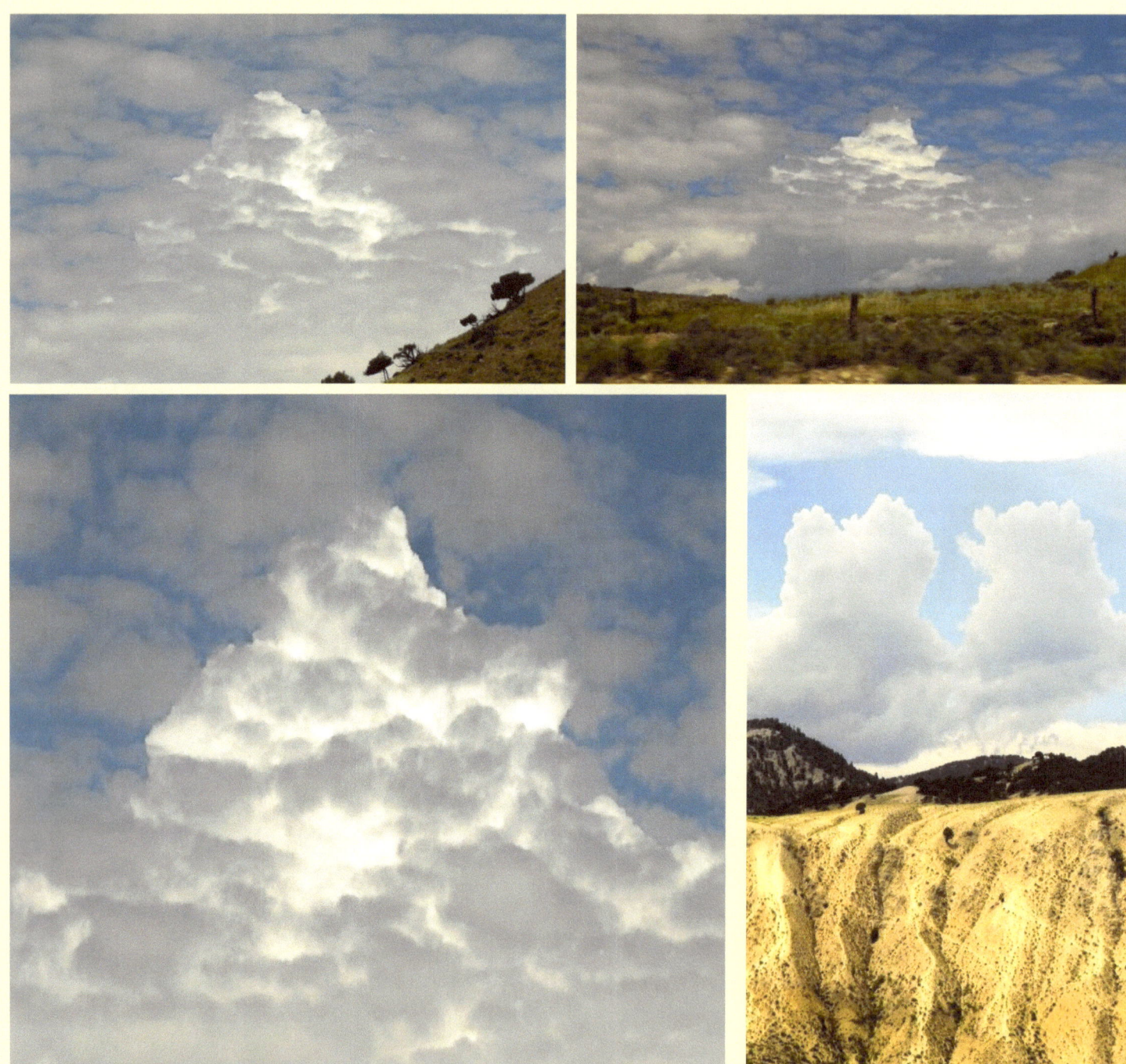

The train winds over, around,
and through the spine of this continent –

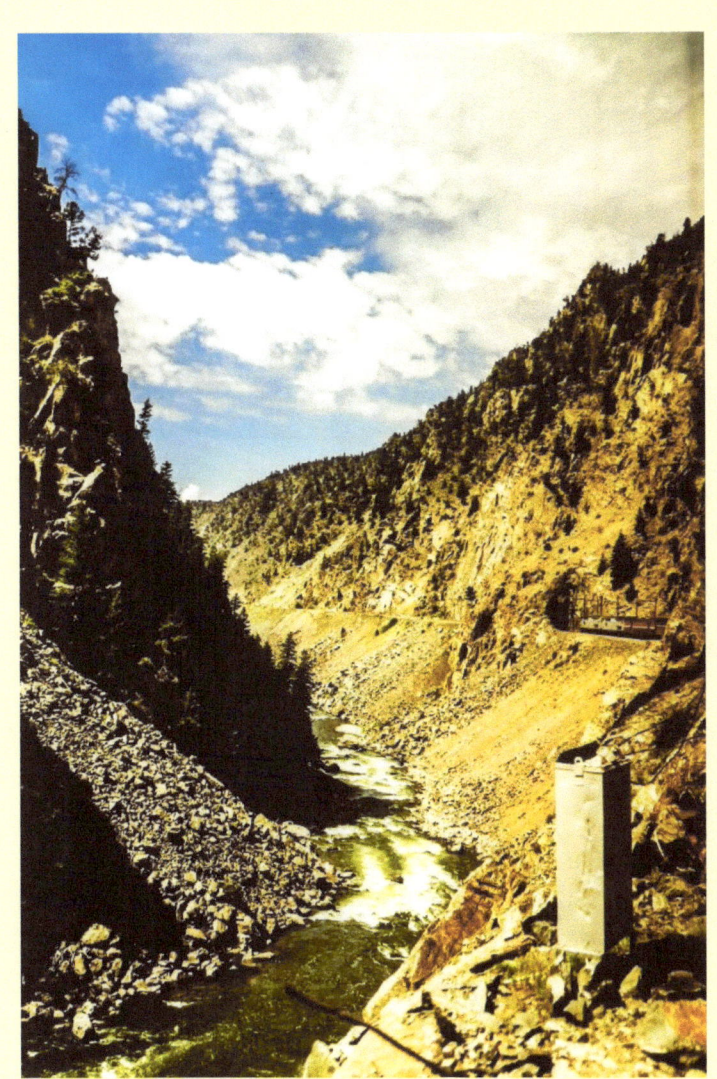

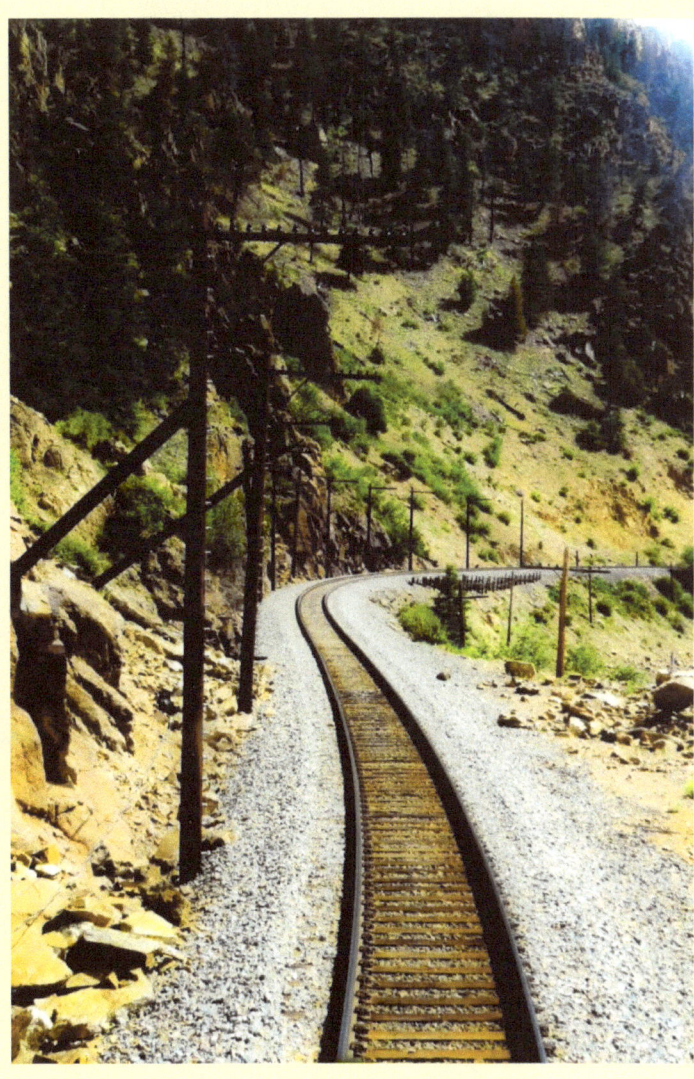

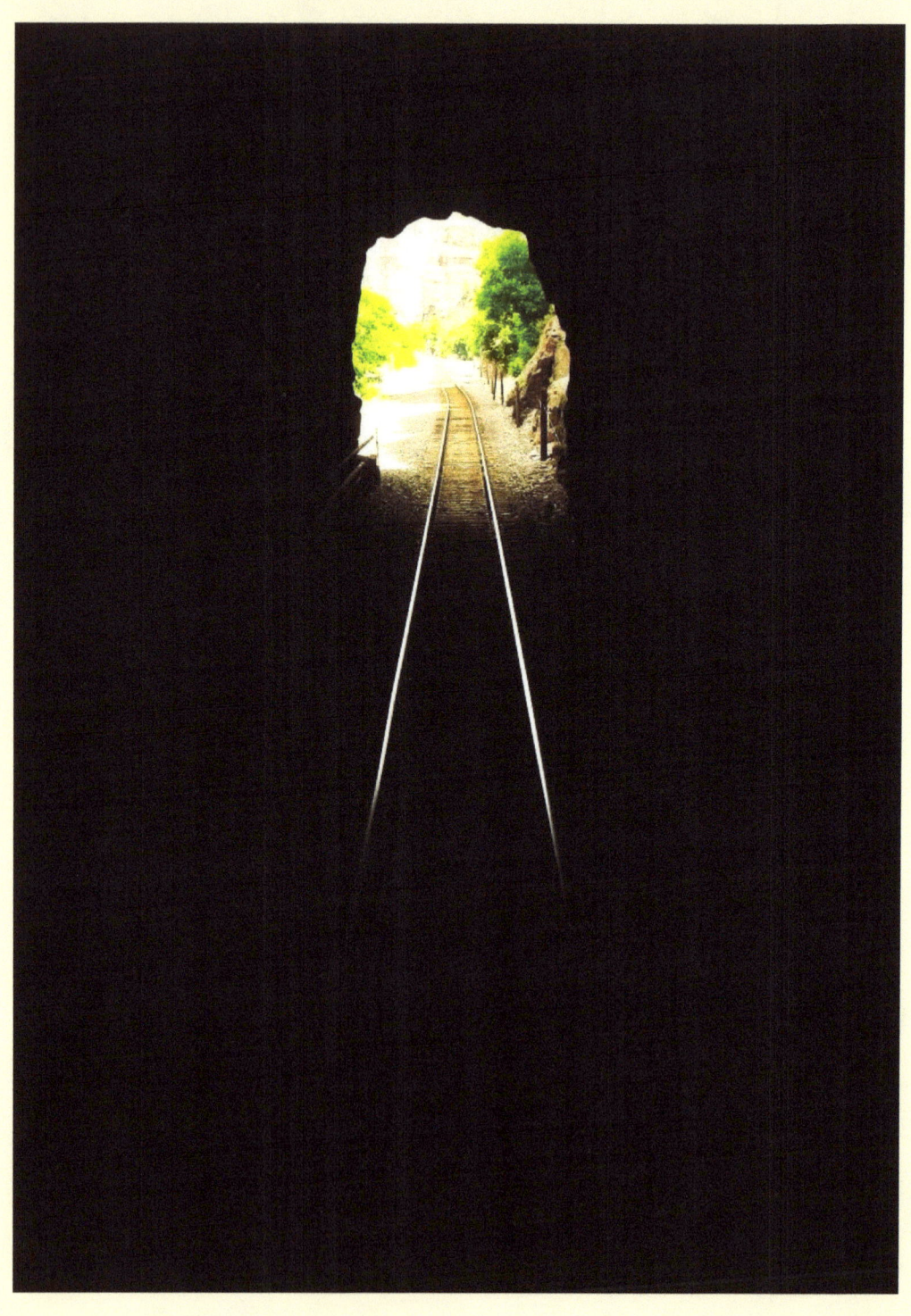

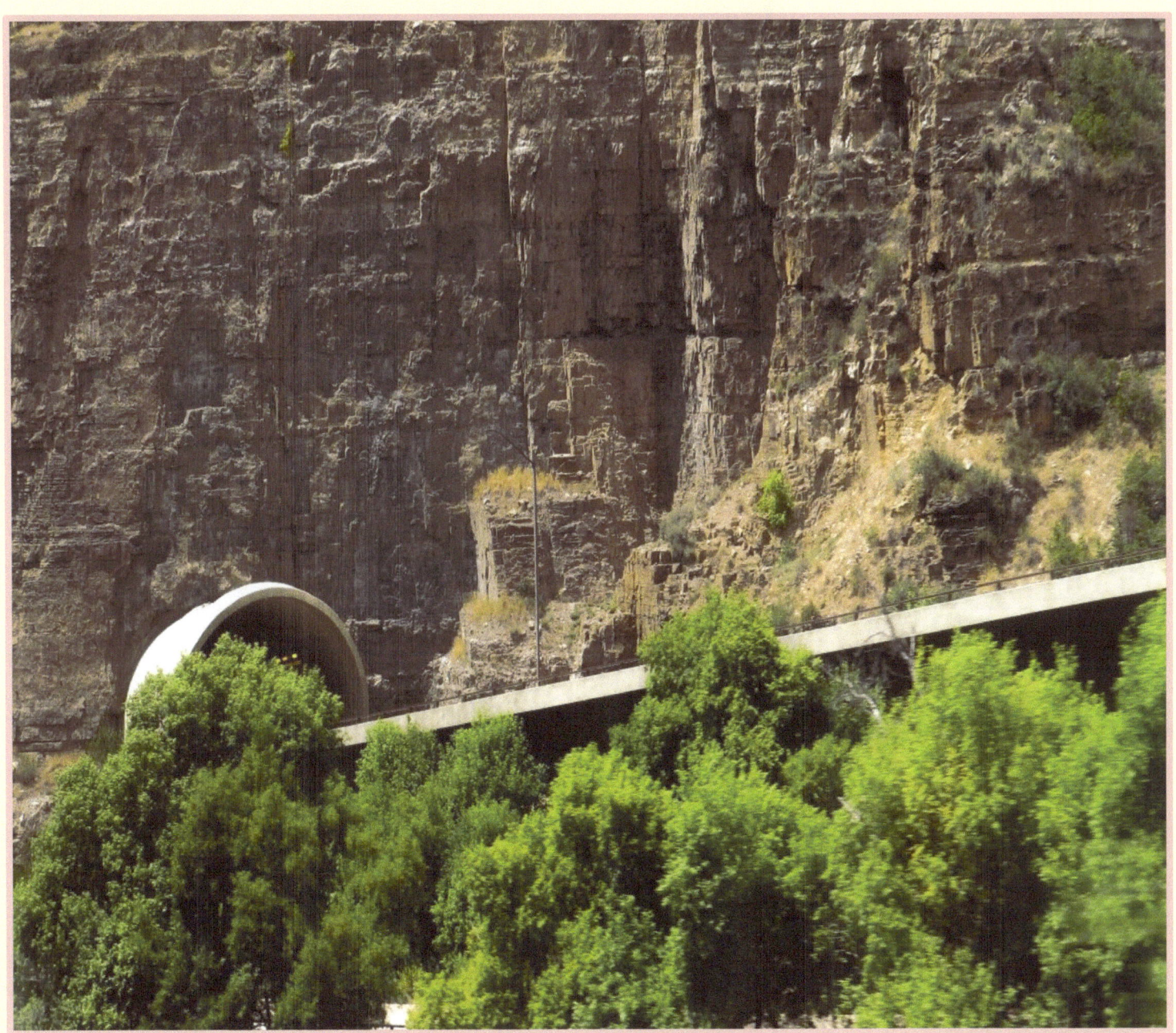

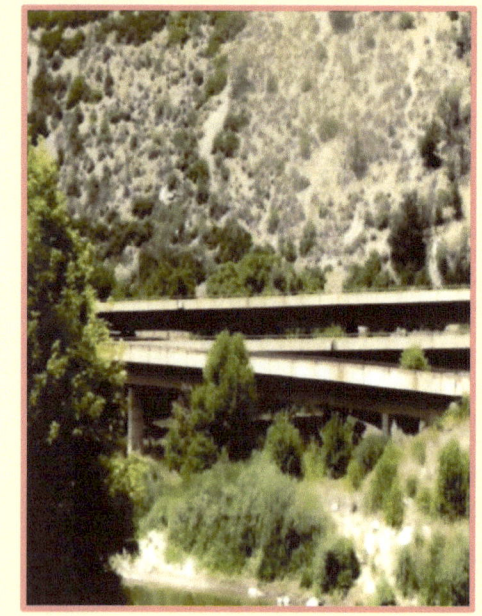

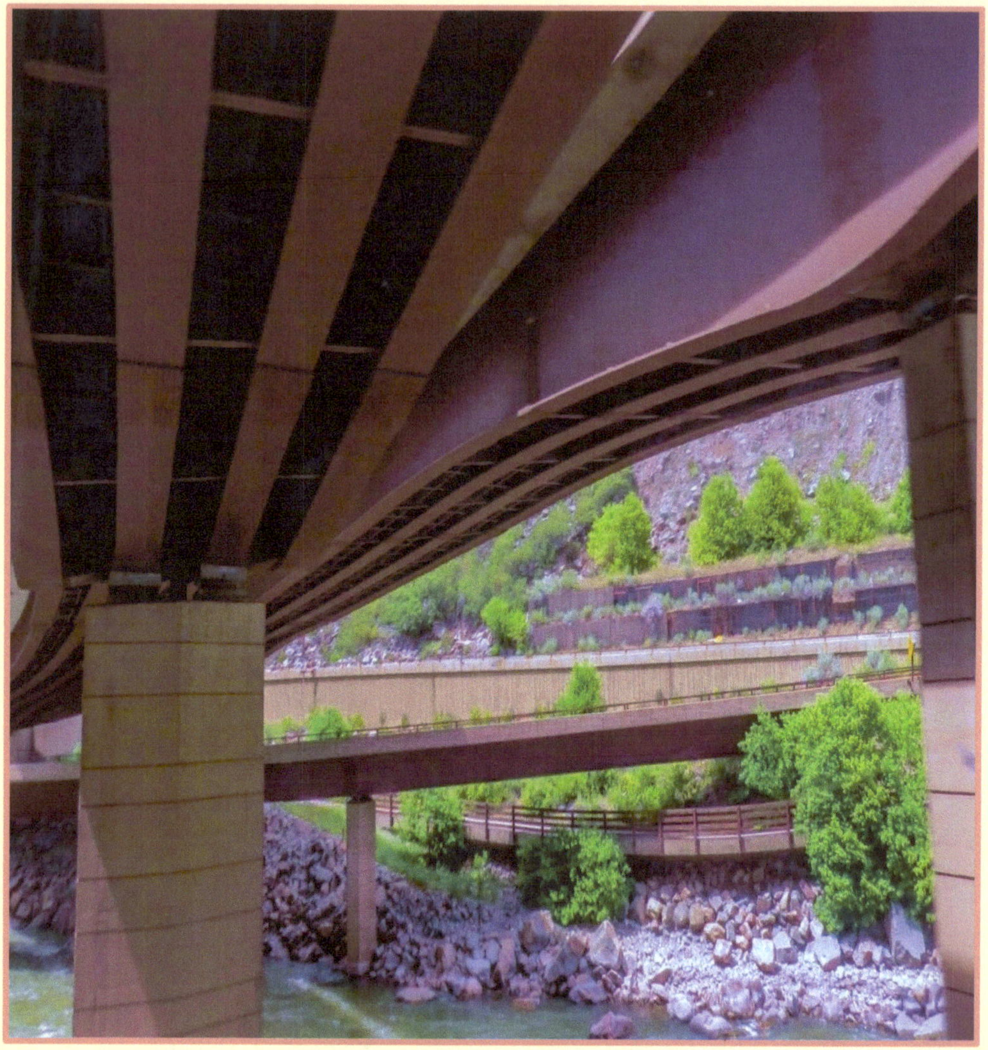

Cross-country journeys today
are not at all what mountain men encountered
– Nor the families of 10,000 years before –

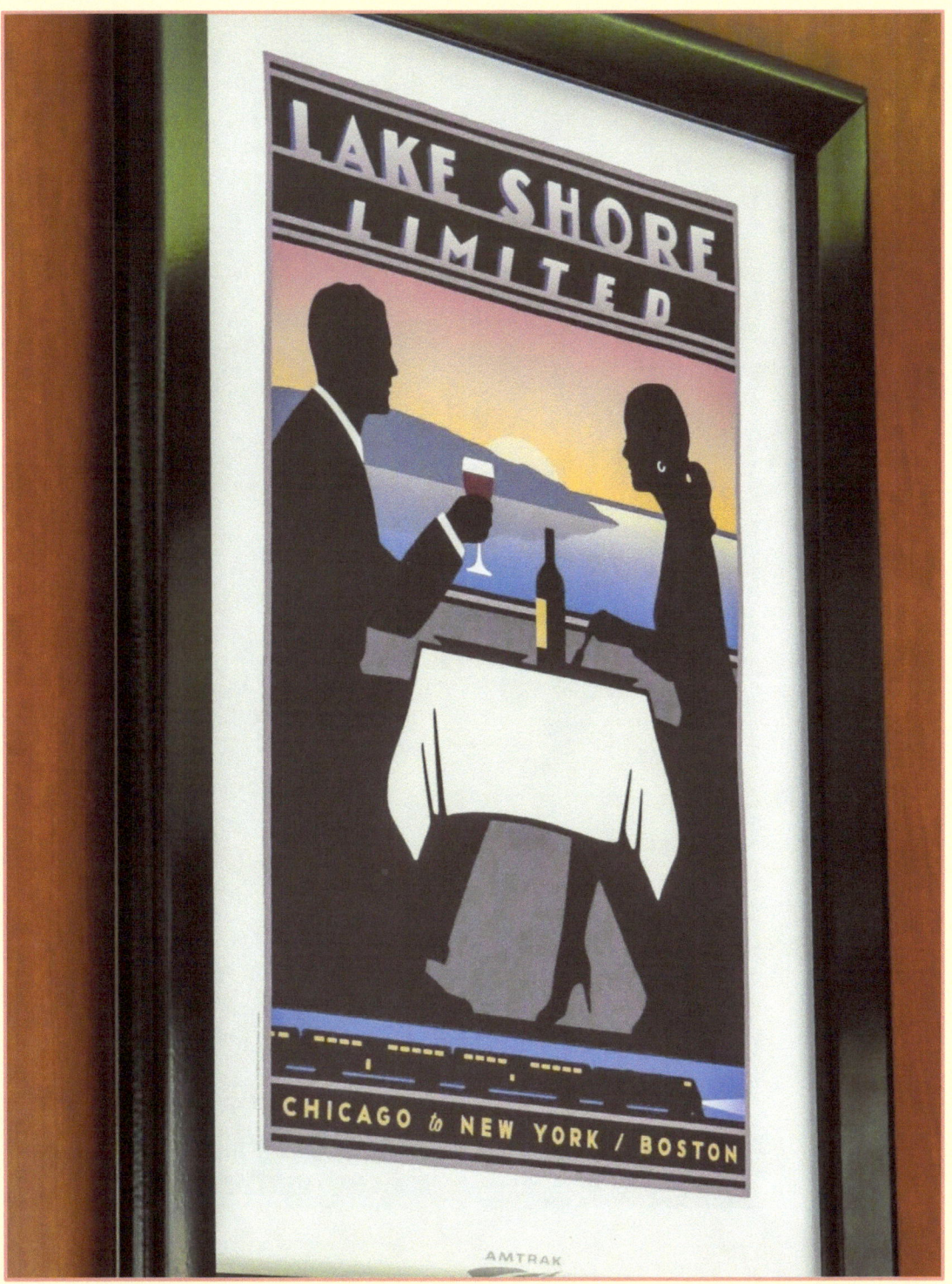

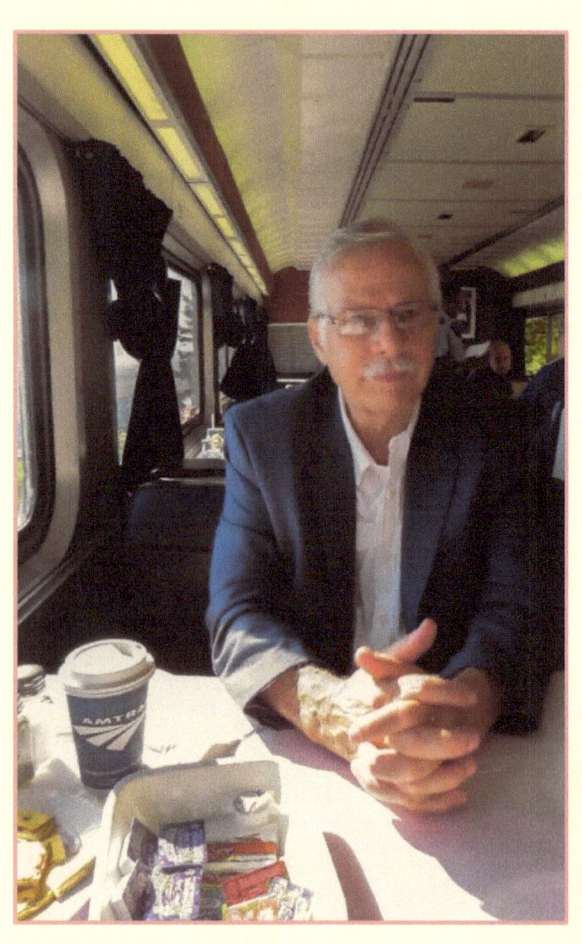

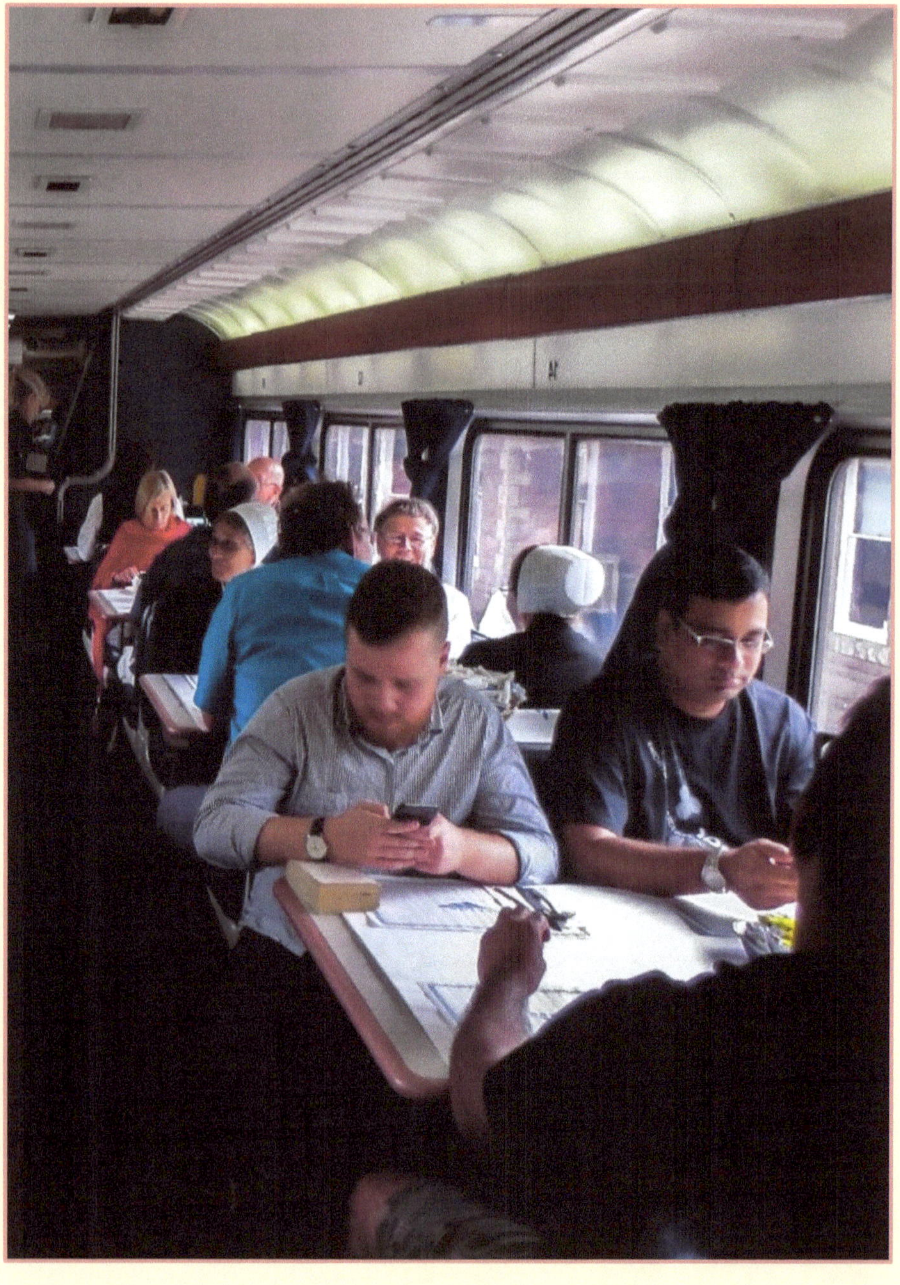

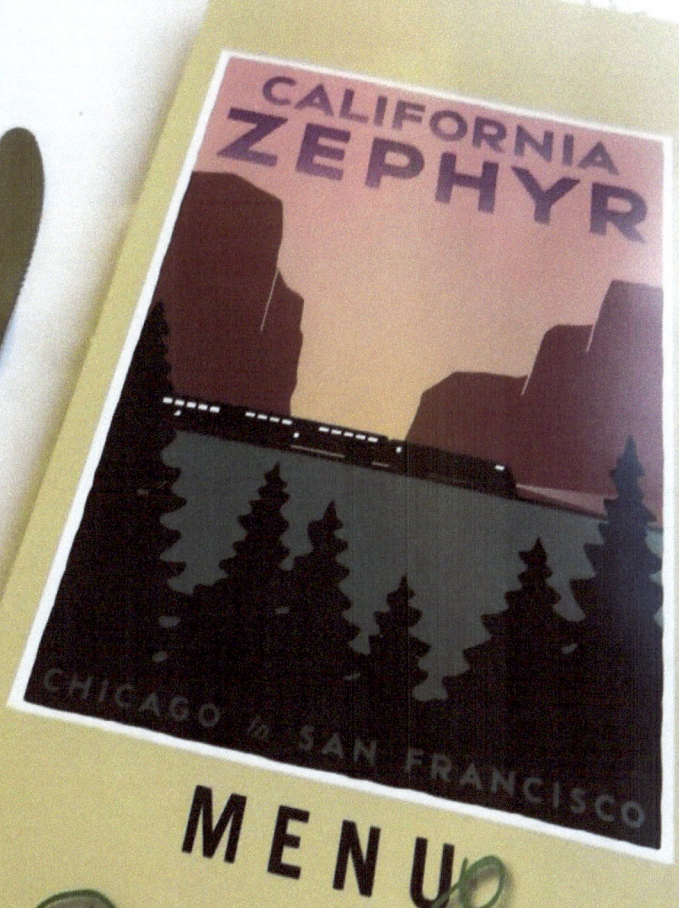

CALIFORNIA ZEPHYR

CHICAGO to SAN FRANCISCO

MENU

Dining Car

Amtrak.com

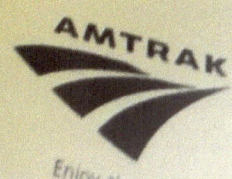

AMTRAK

Enjoy the journey

Glenwood Springs – Roosevelt's famed hunting lair –
boasts geothermal streams
filling-in pools between monumental mountains –

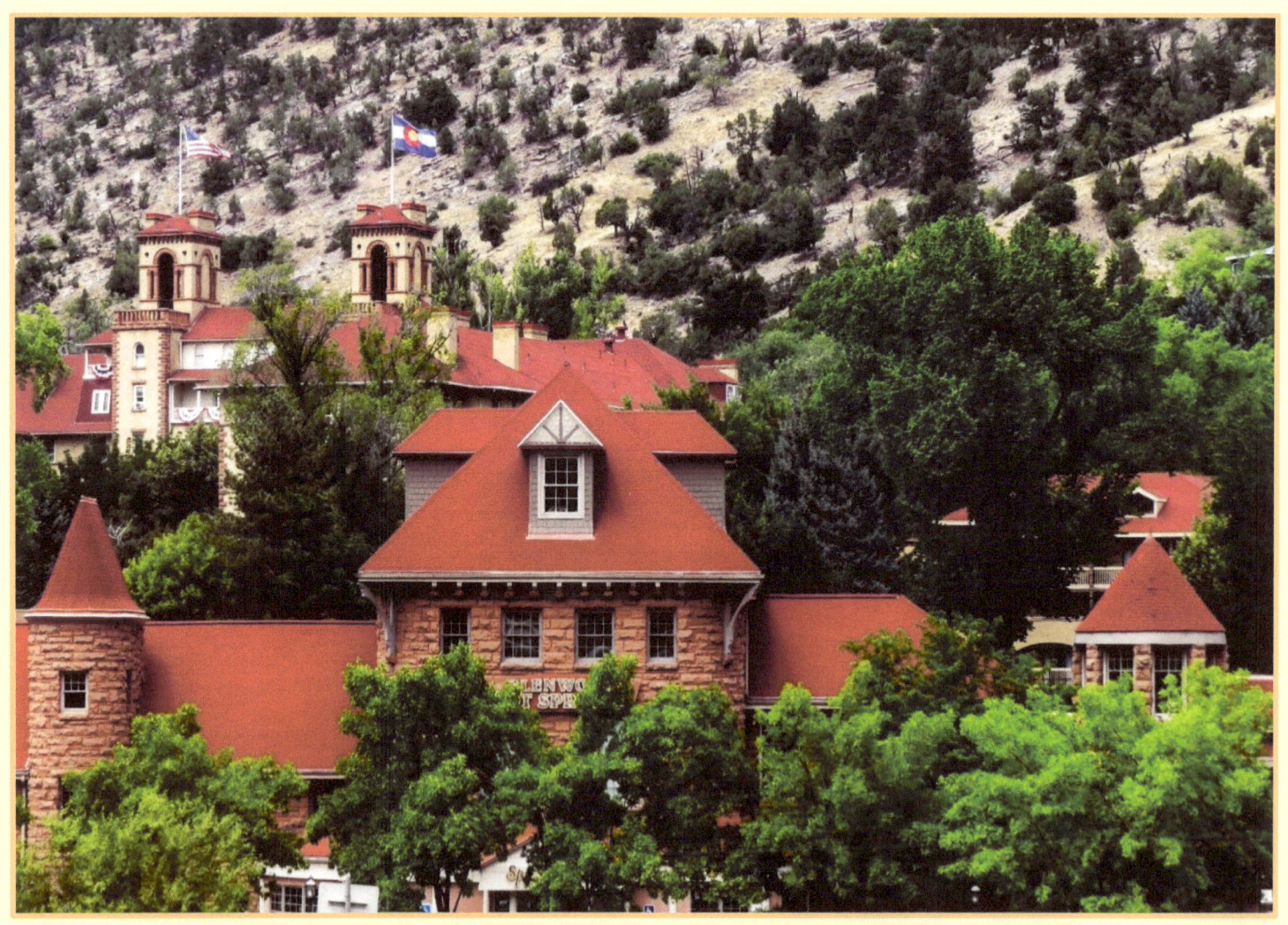

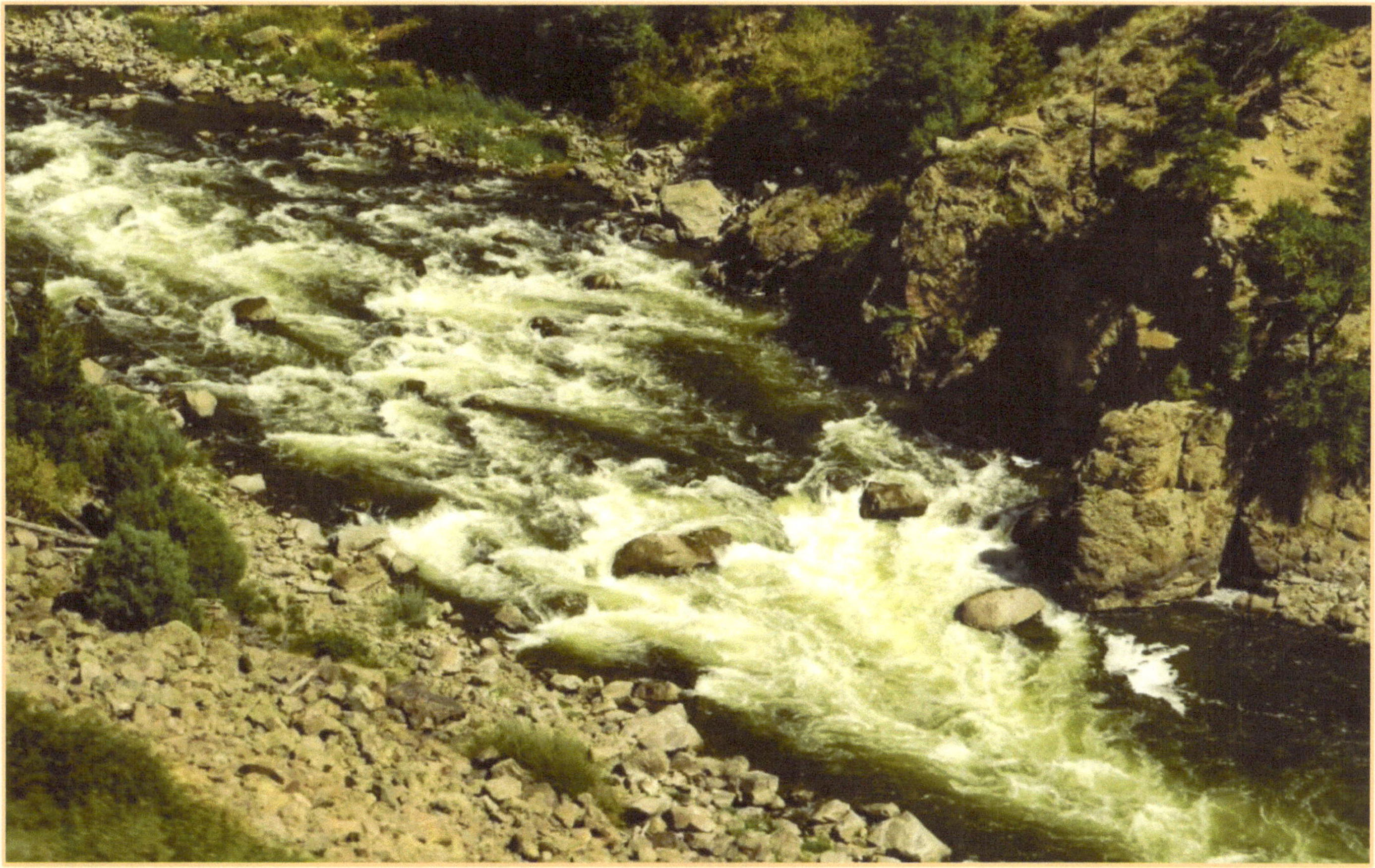

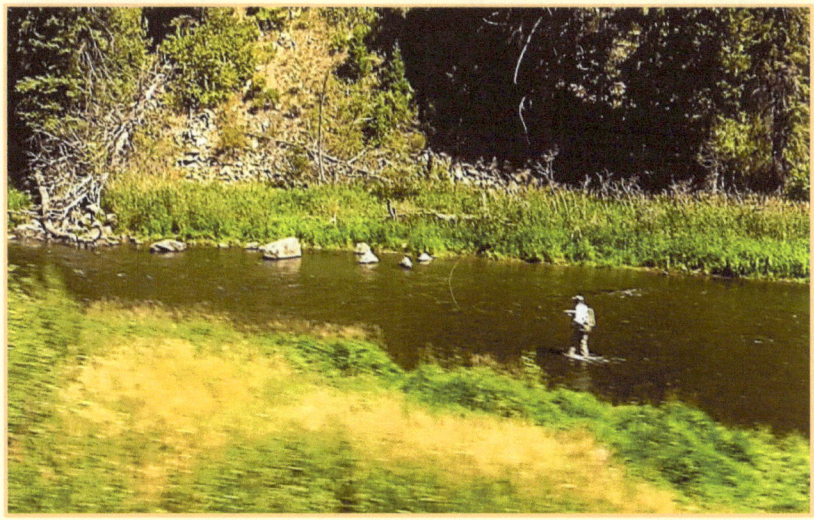
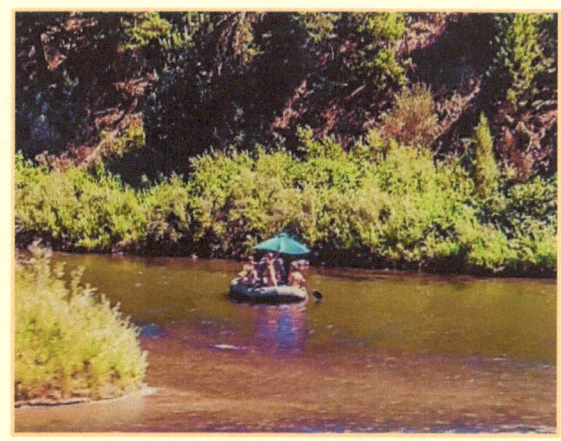

to spawn
fishing
and floating
activities
galore –

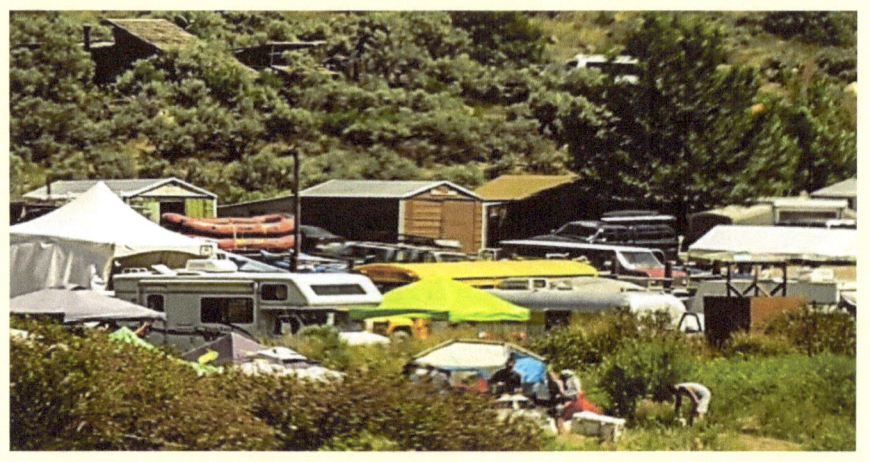

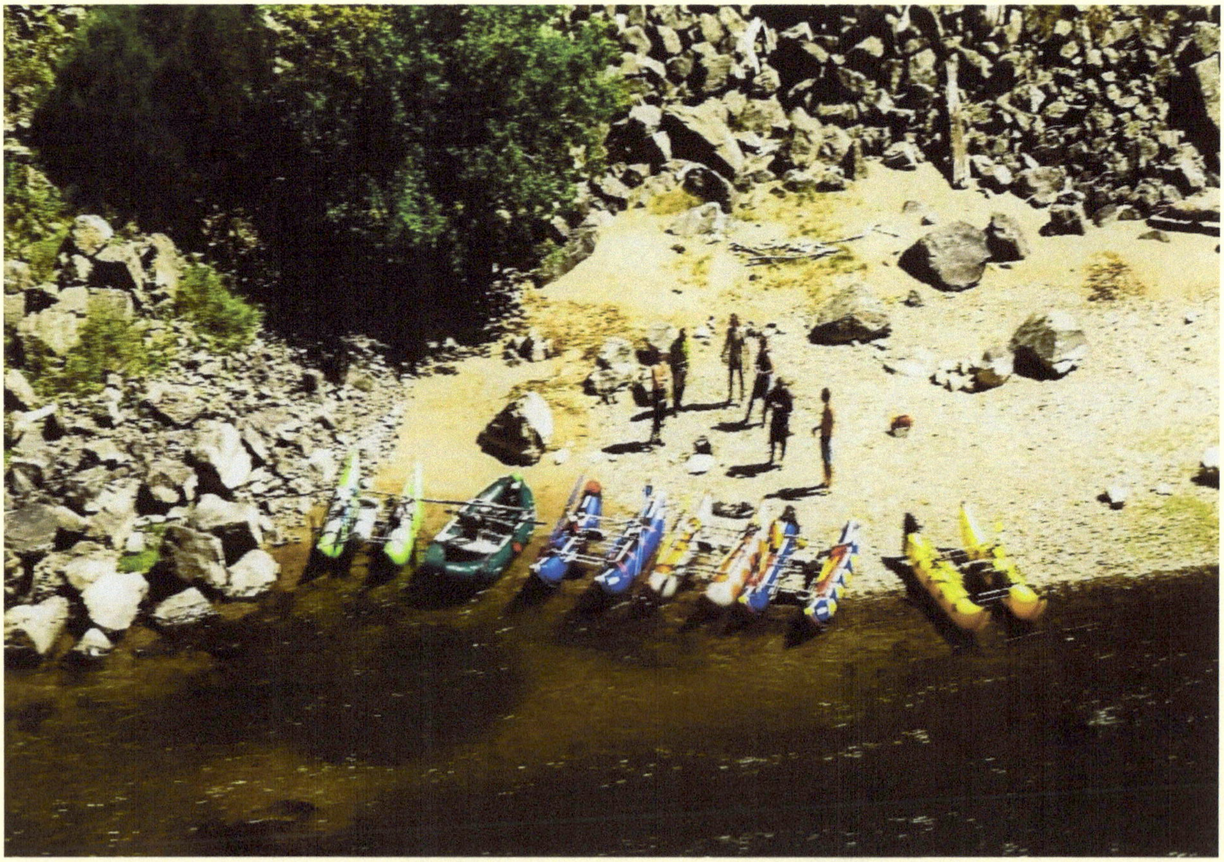

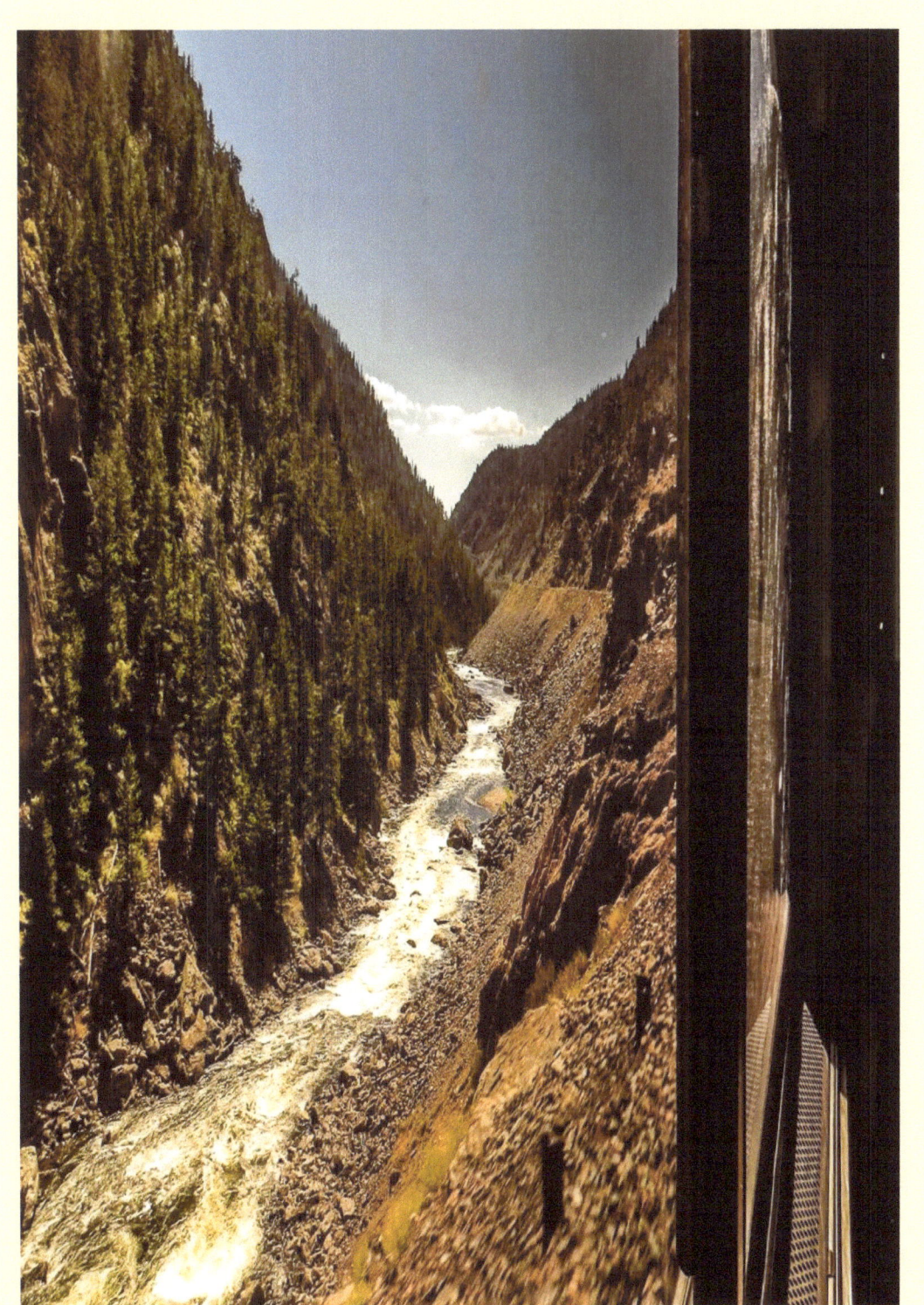

The
Colorado River
is well-
utilized
by those on the
western slope –

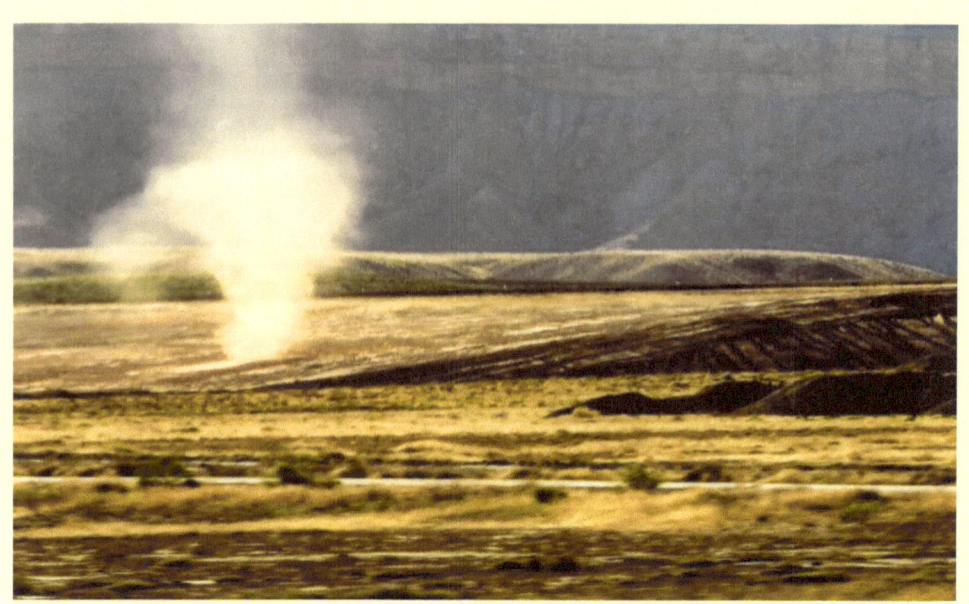
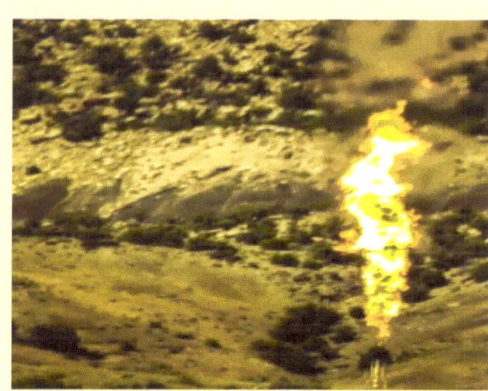

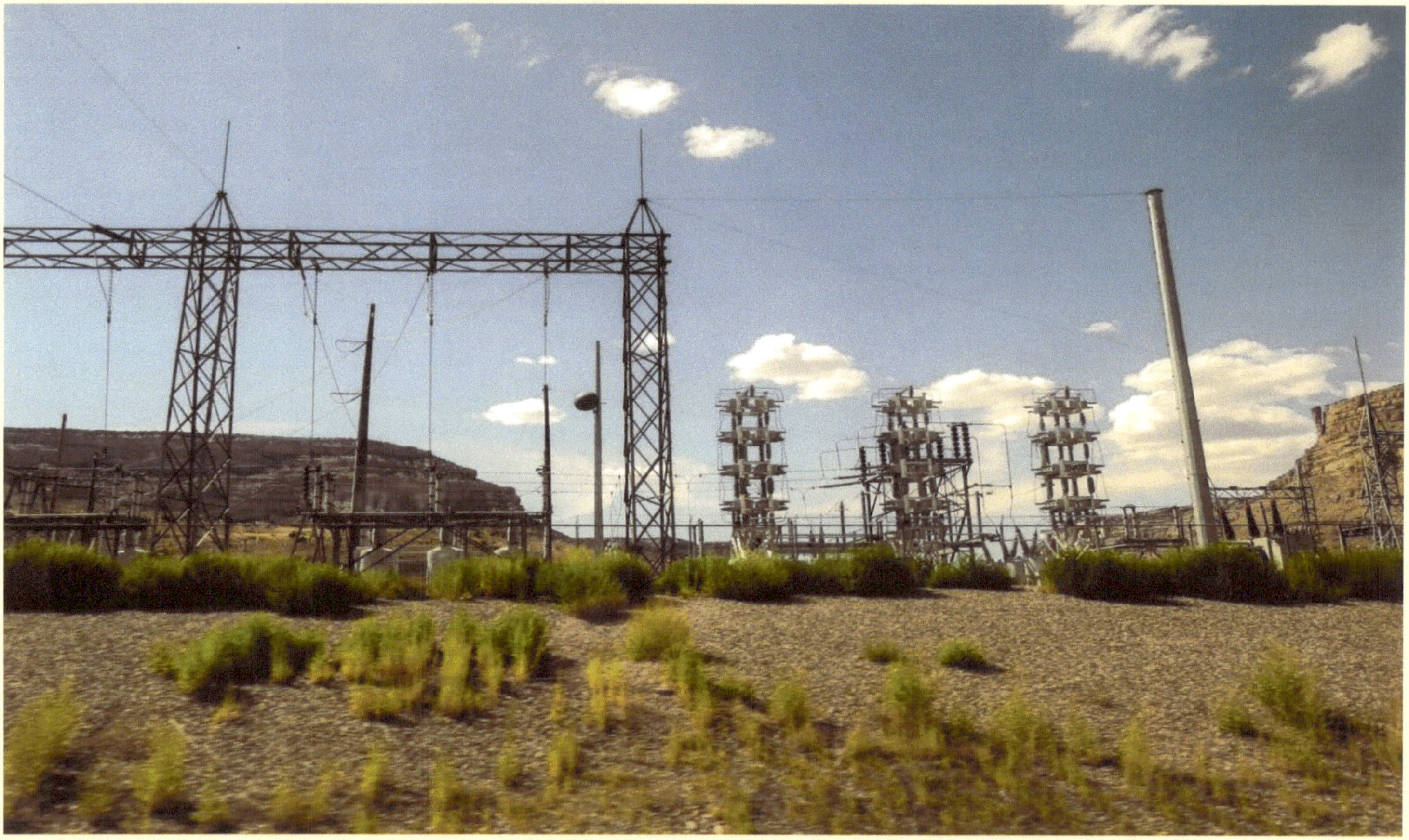

Even when the Colorado turns away, to head south –

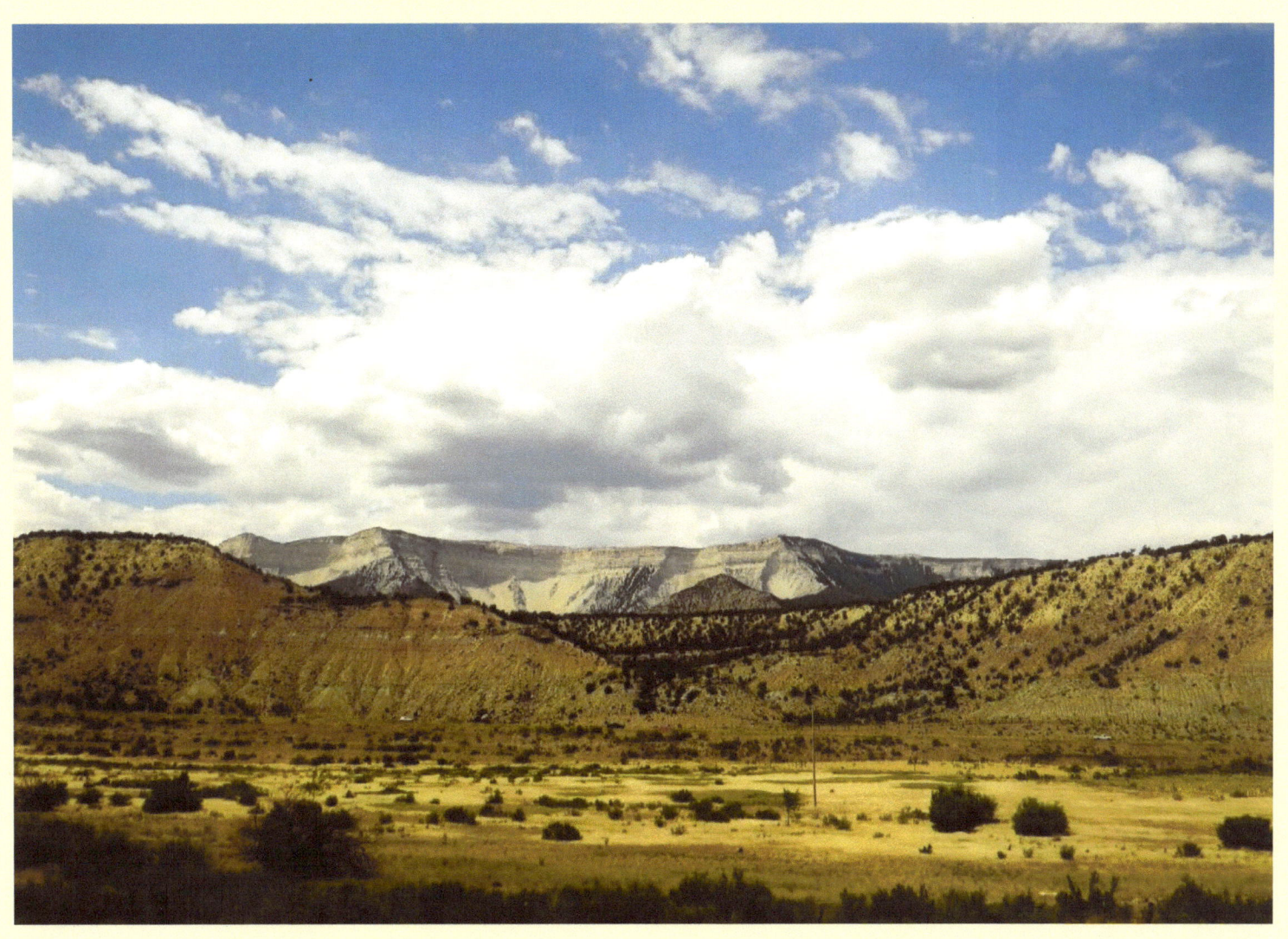

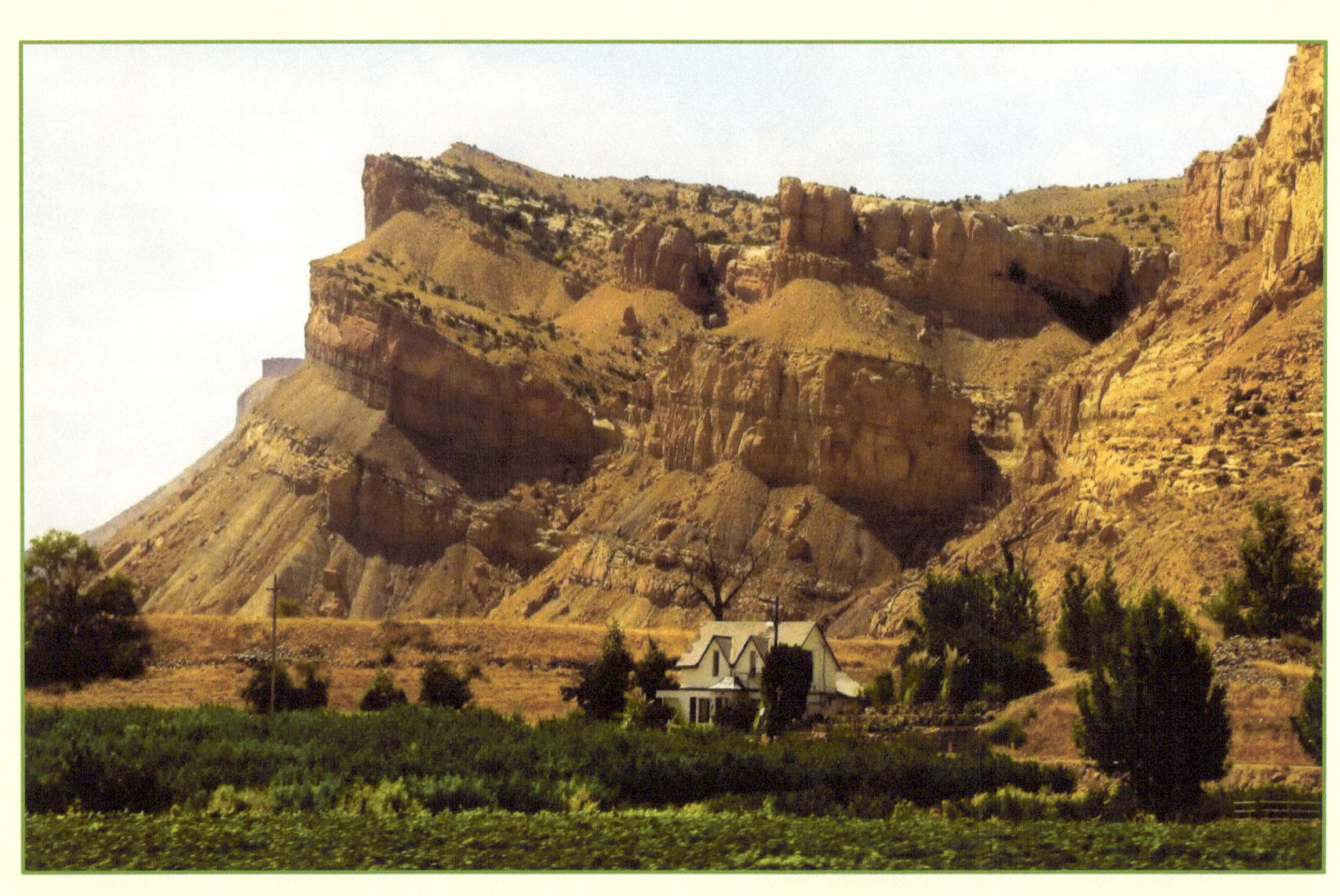

Northern Utah is well-managed and plush –

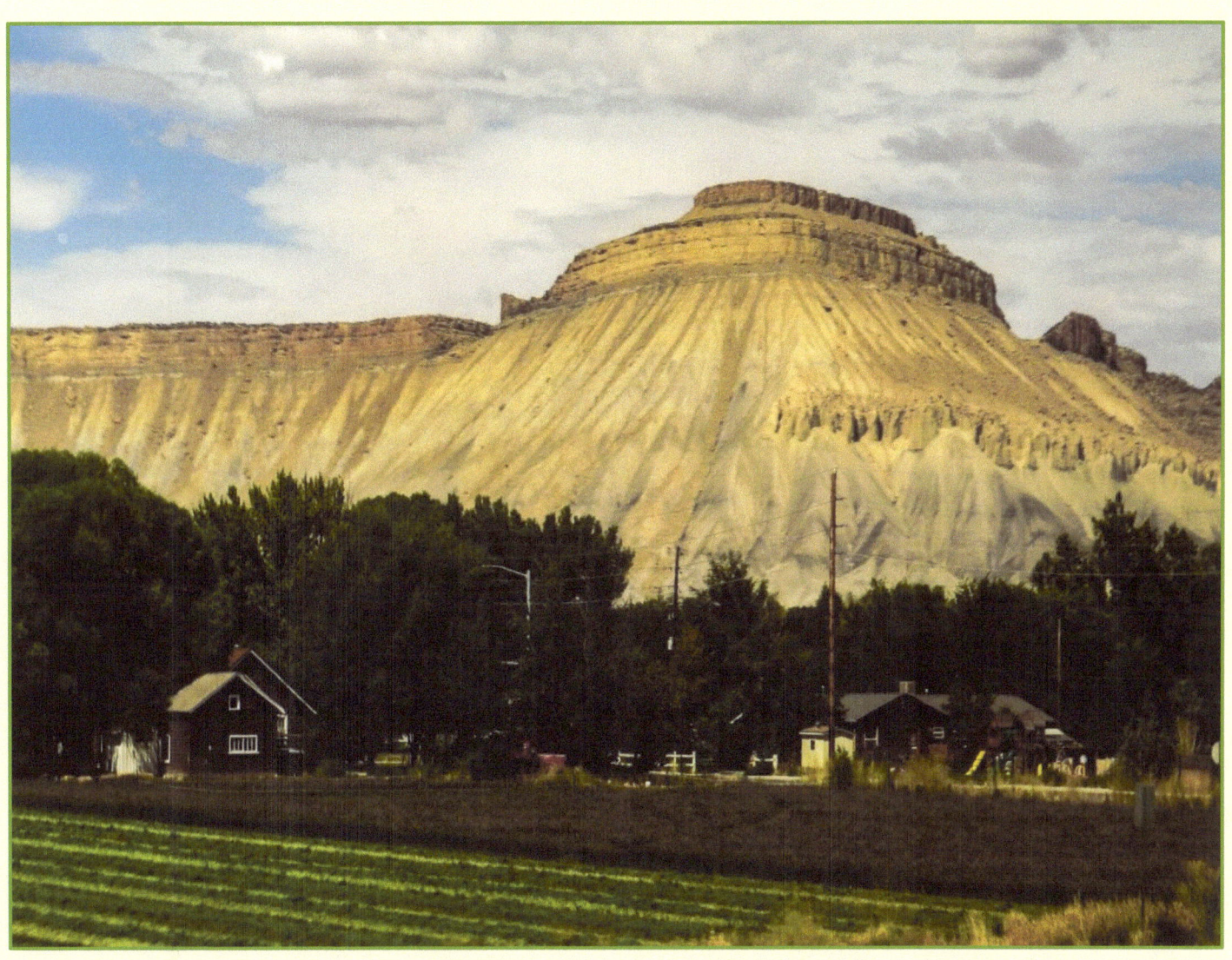

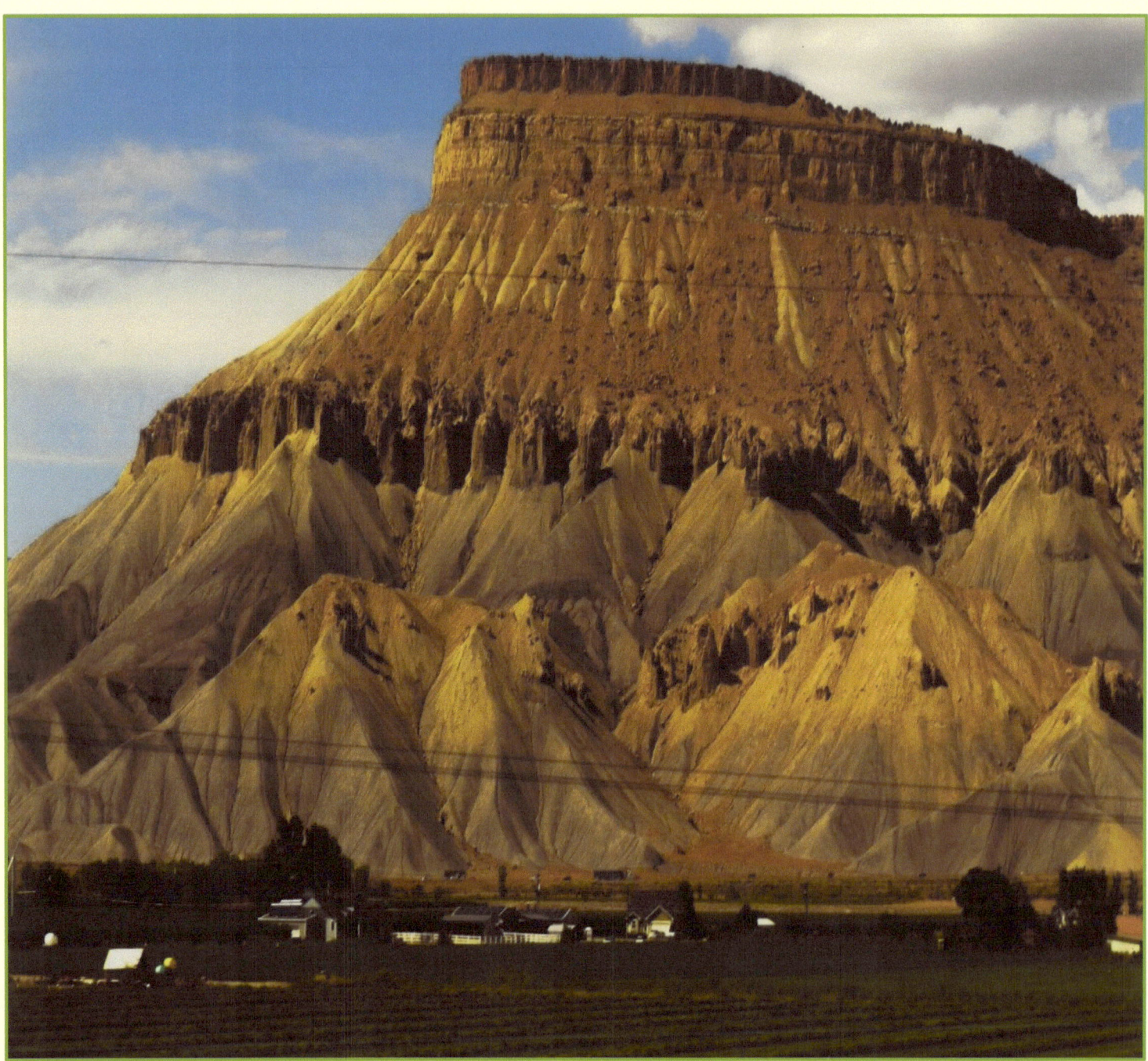

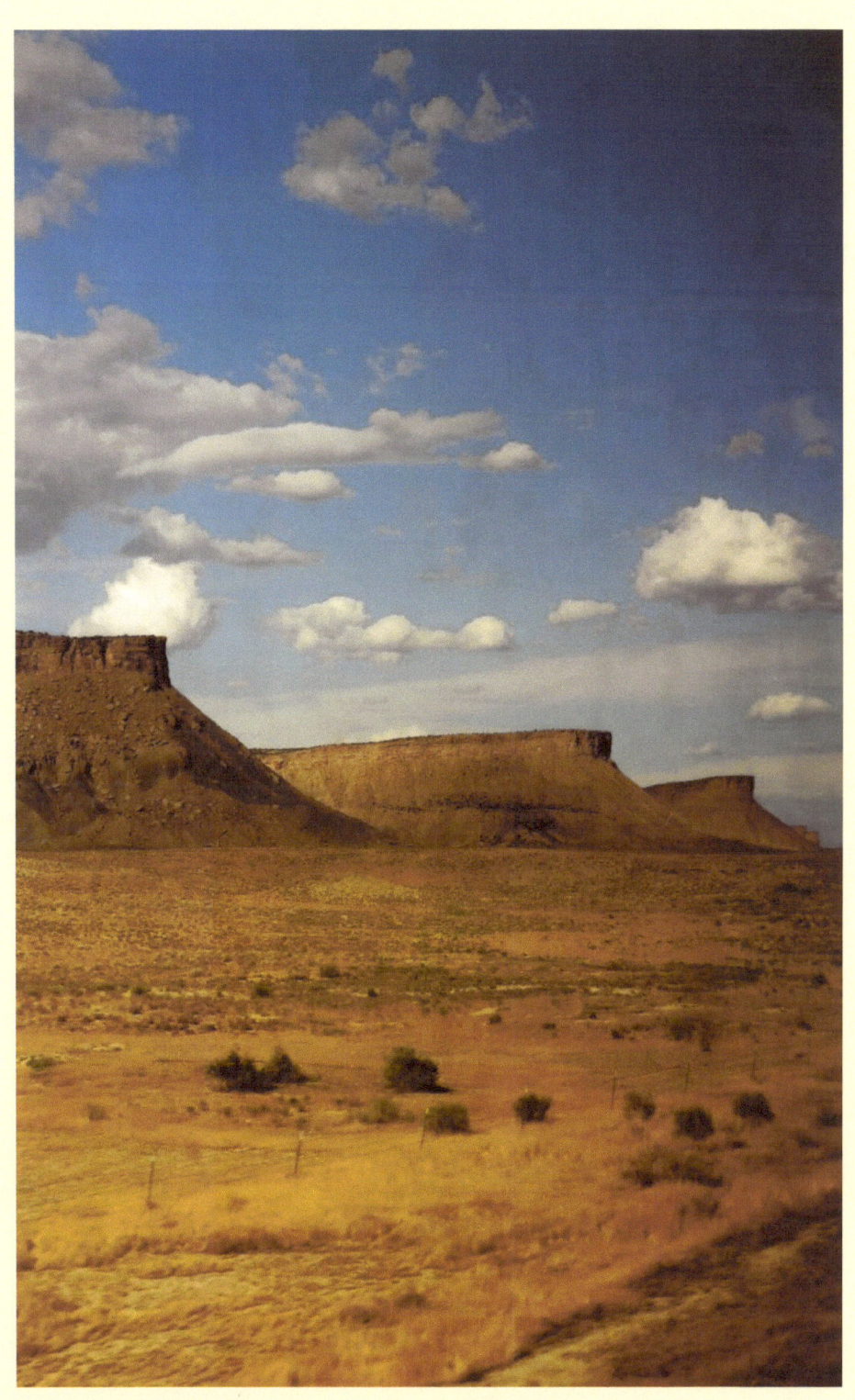

Then,
northern Nevada
is barren,
but beautiful
and
quite unique —

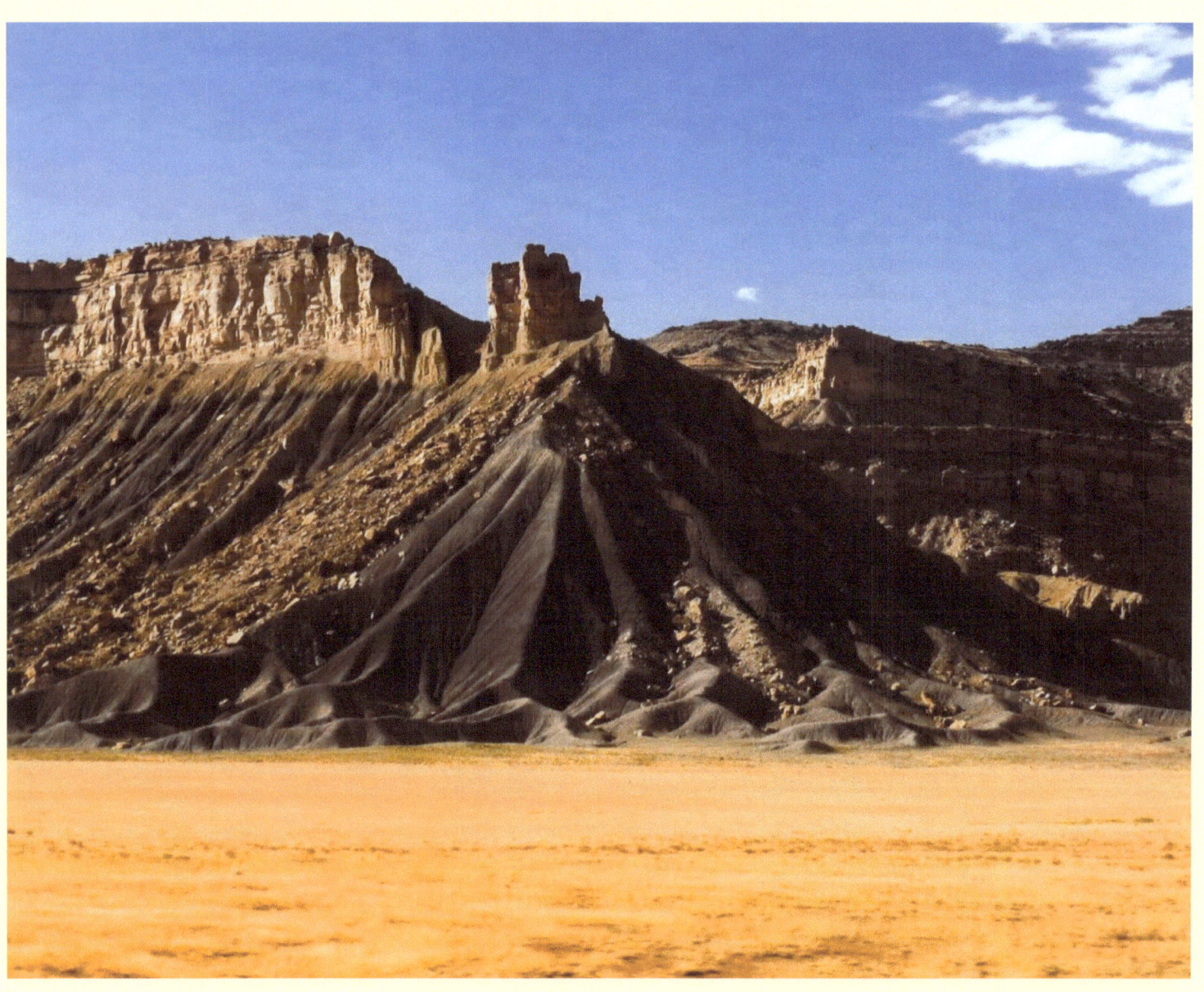

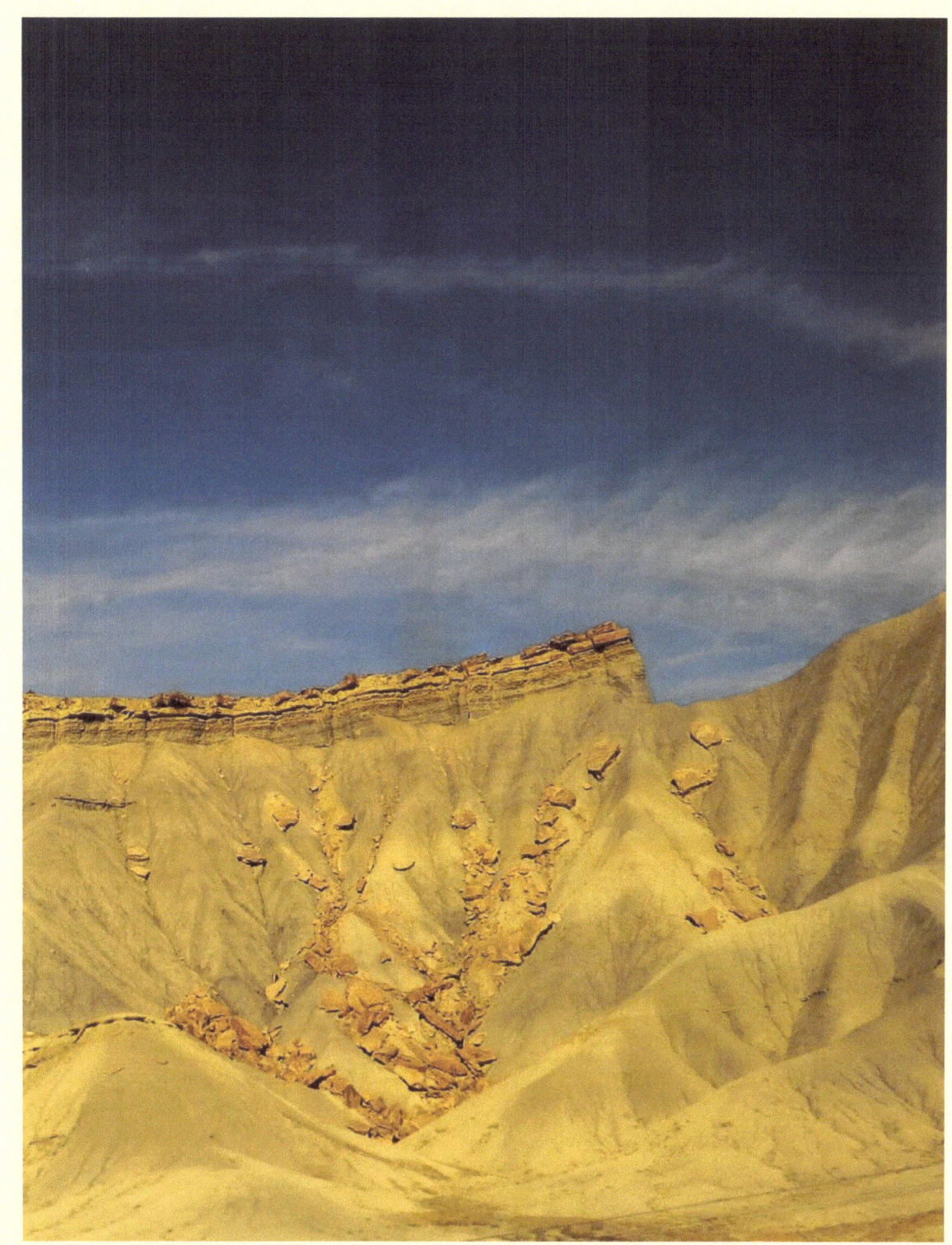

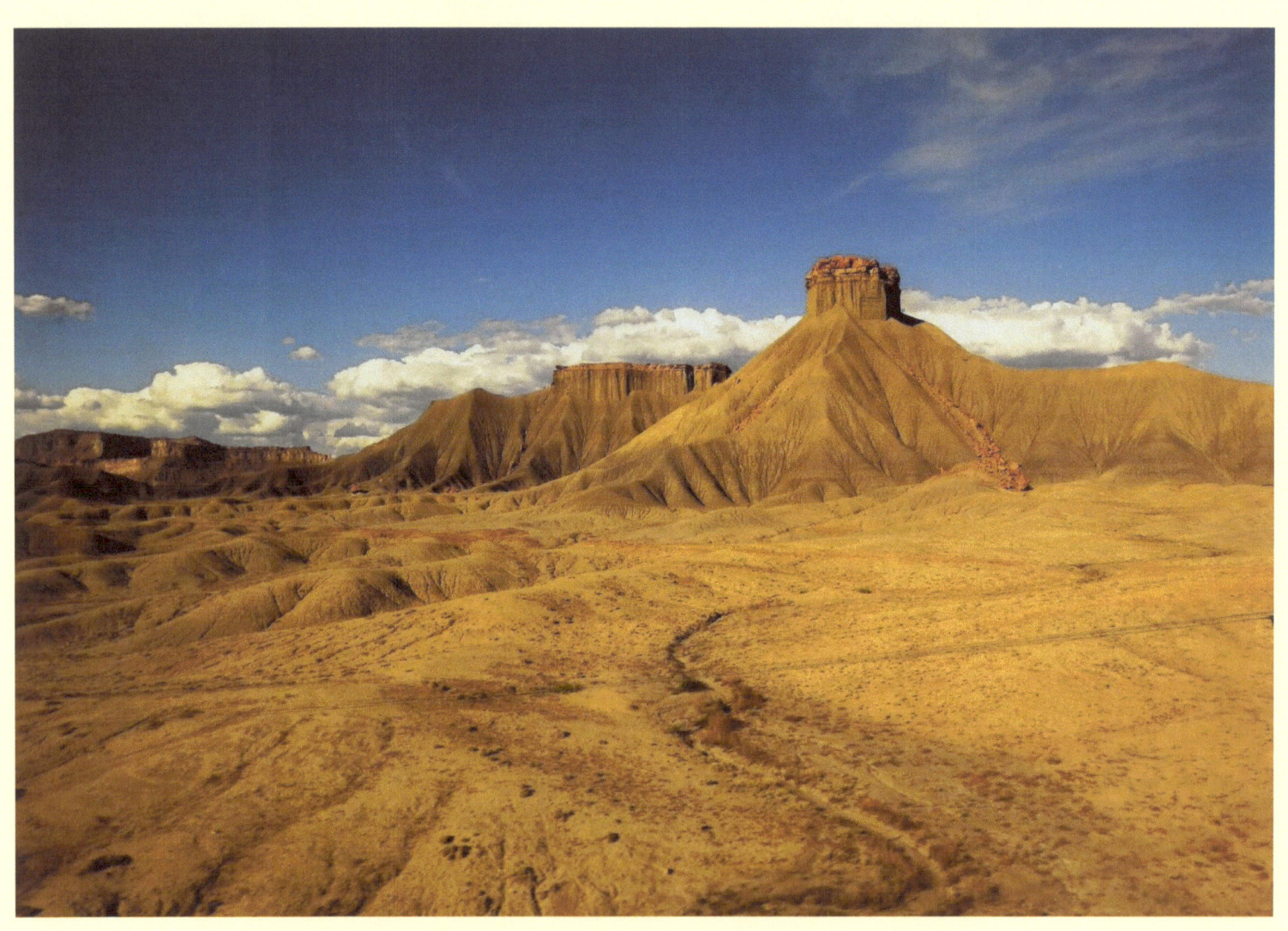

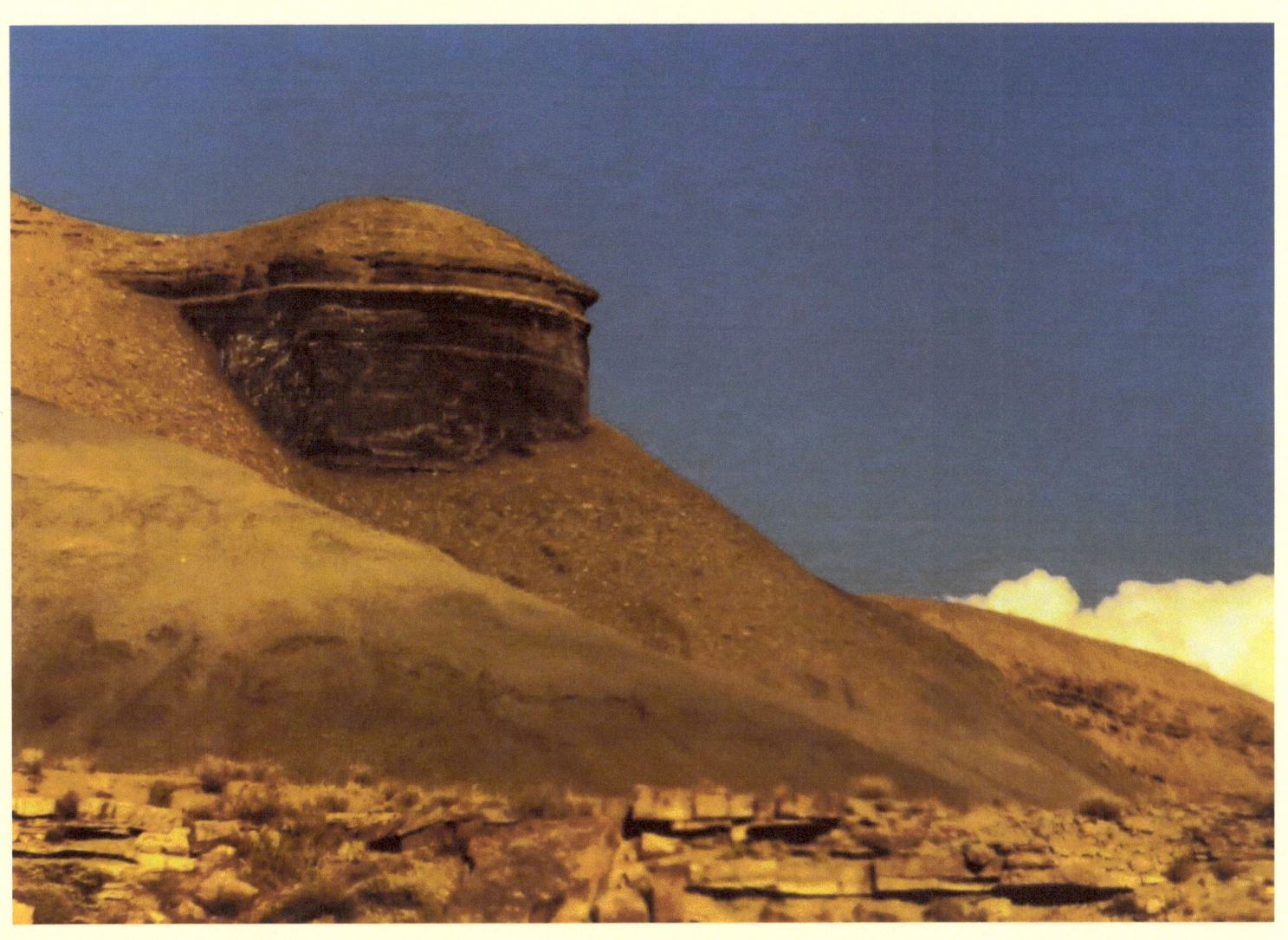

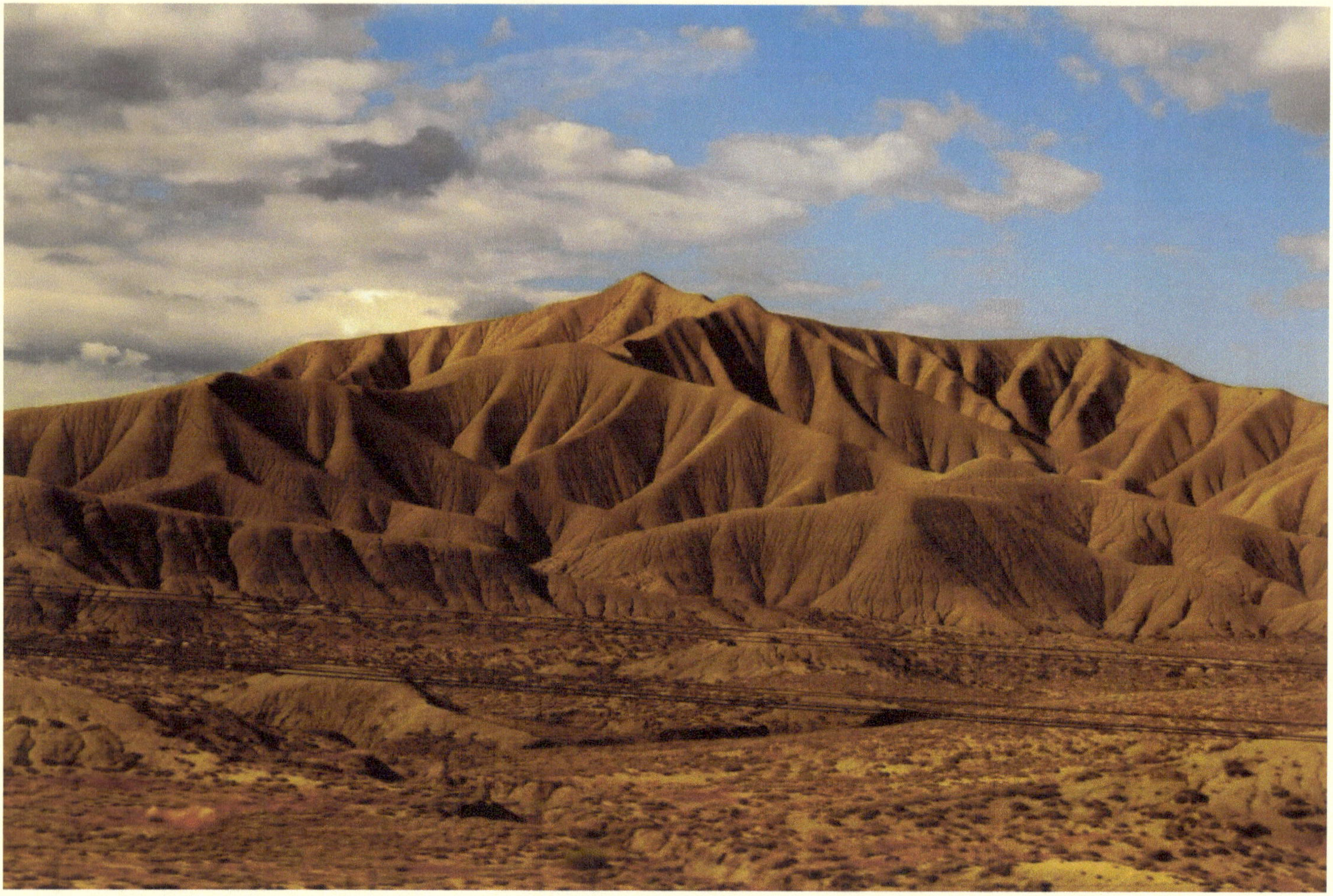

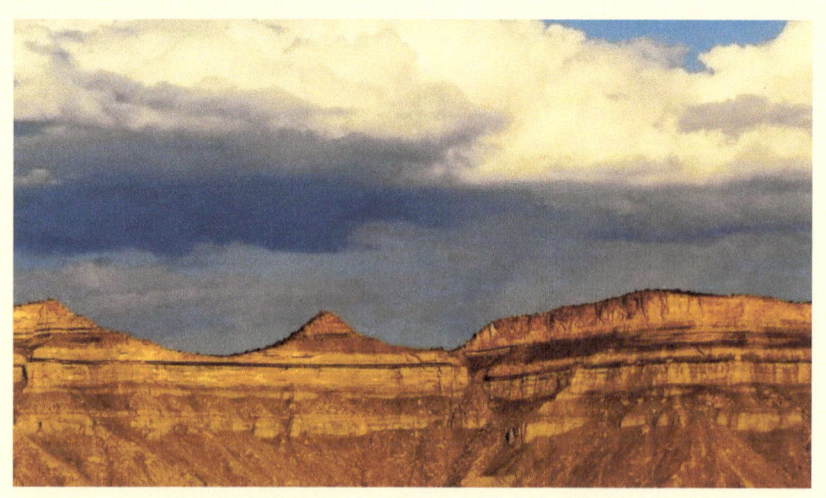

With its
haunting mountains
subtly folded
and oddly eroded
– to perfect effect –

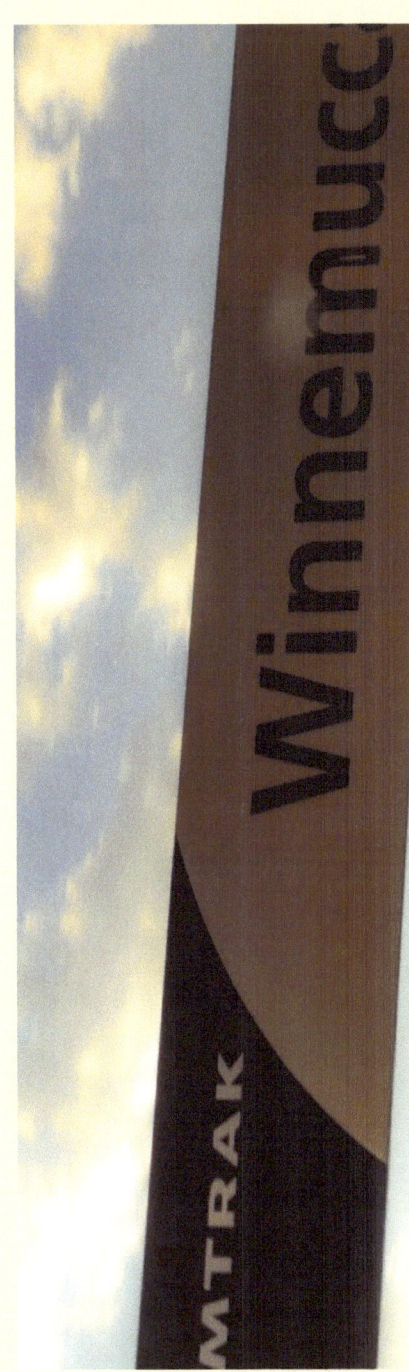

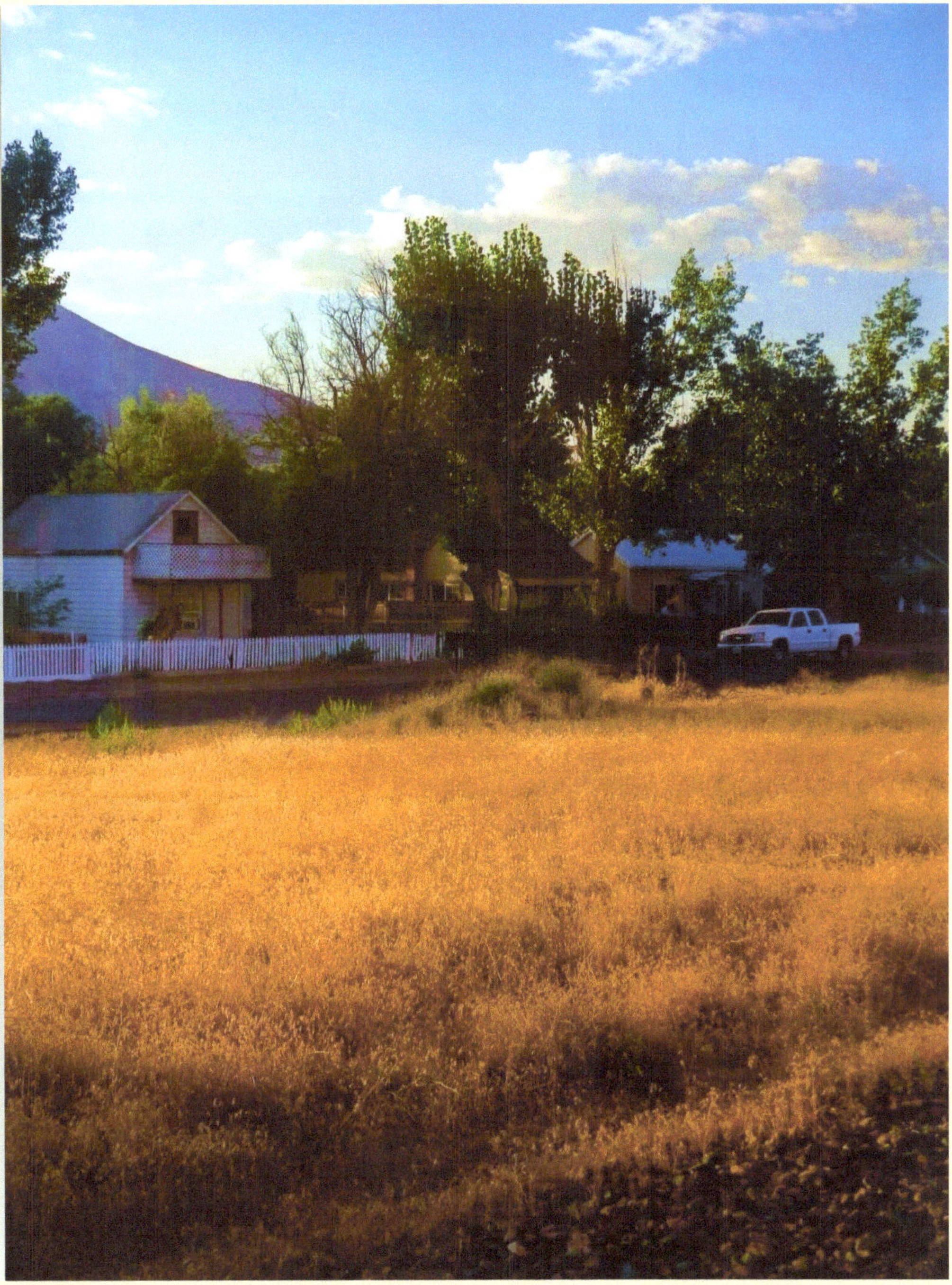

Winnemucca, once a resting place on the California Trail –

Offers sunsets eaqual to the Southwest Chief's –

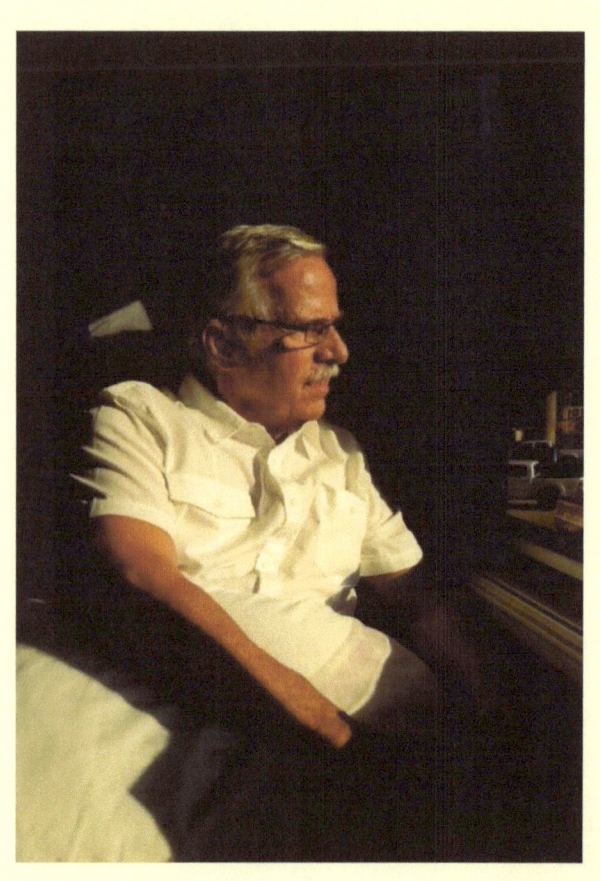

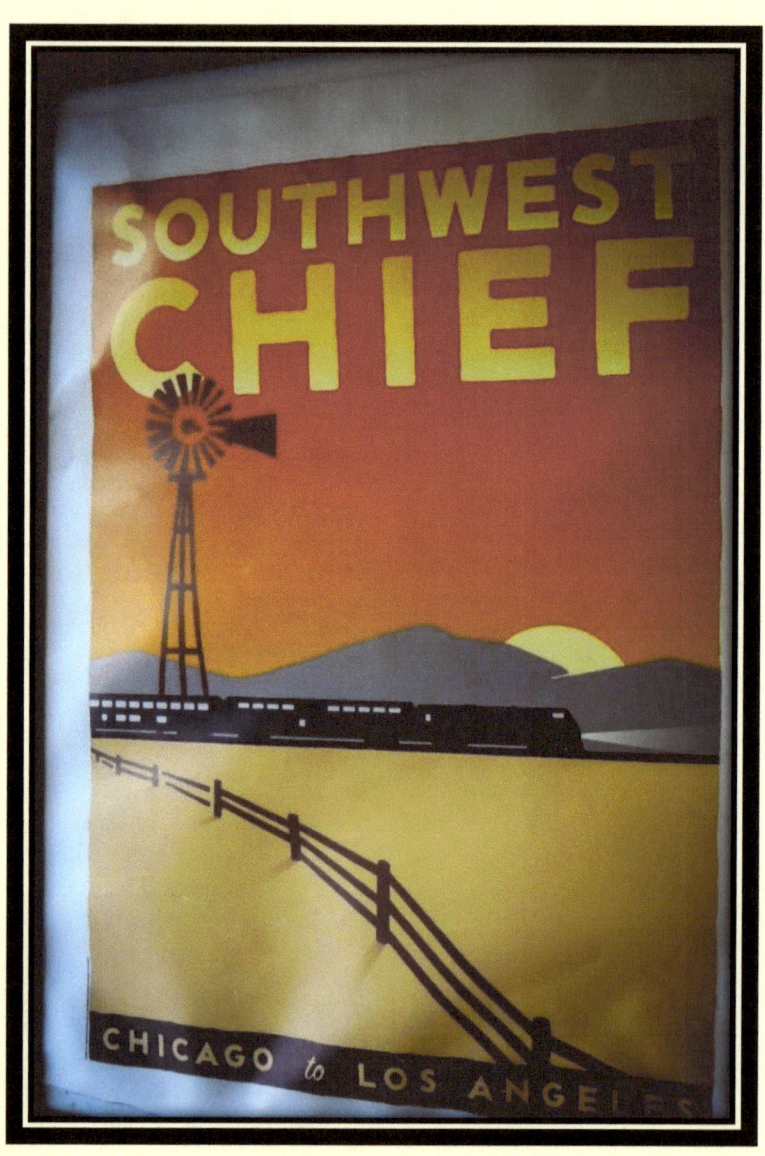

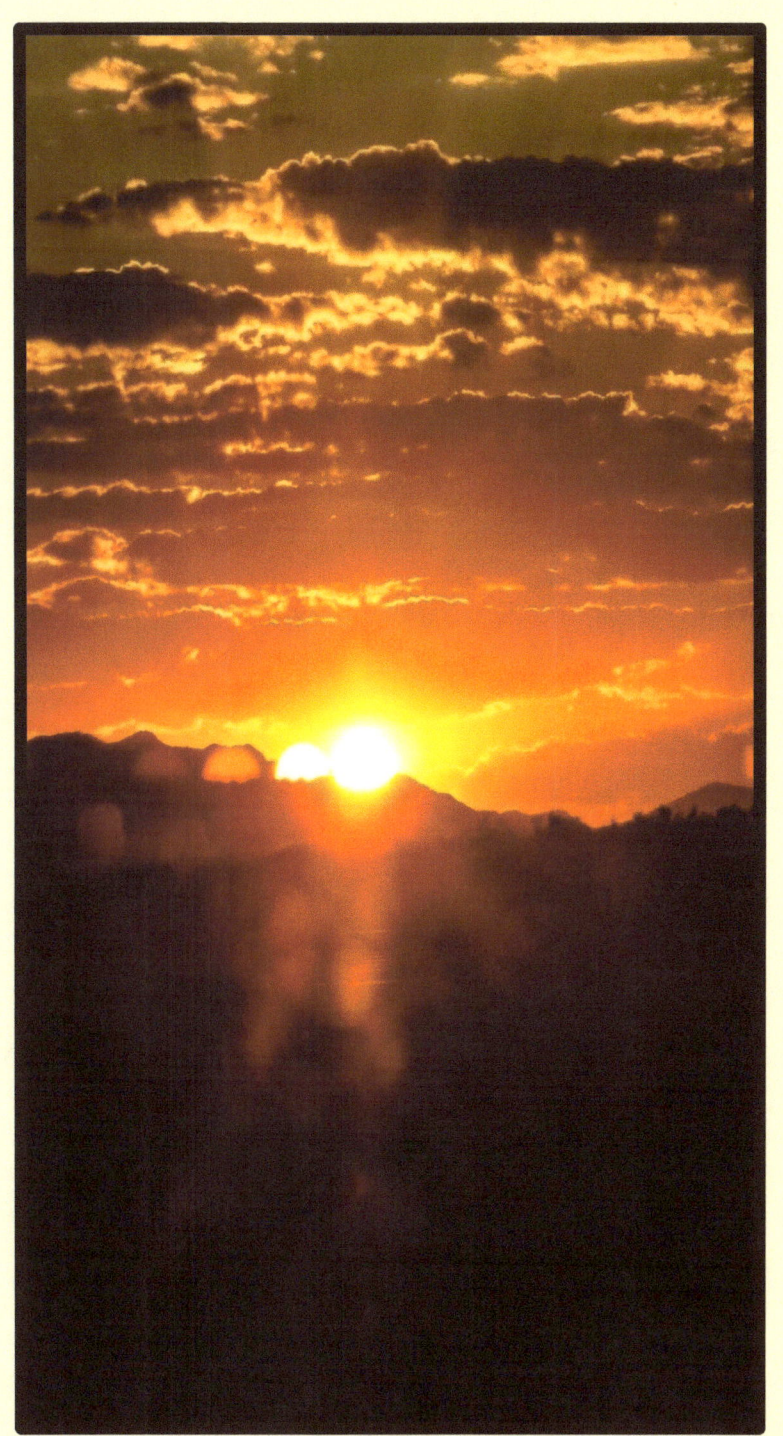

As the Zephyr
and her sister trains
stir nostalgia
in those who have
surrendered themselves
to a slower pace –

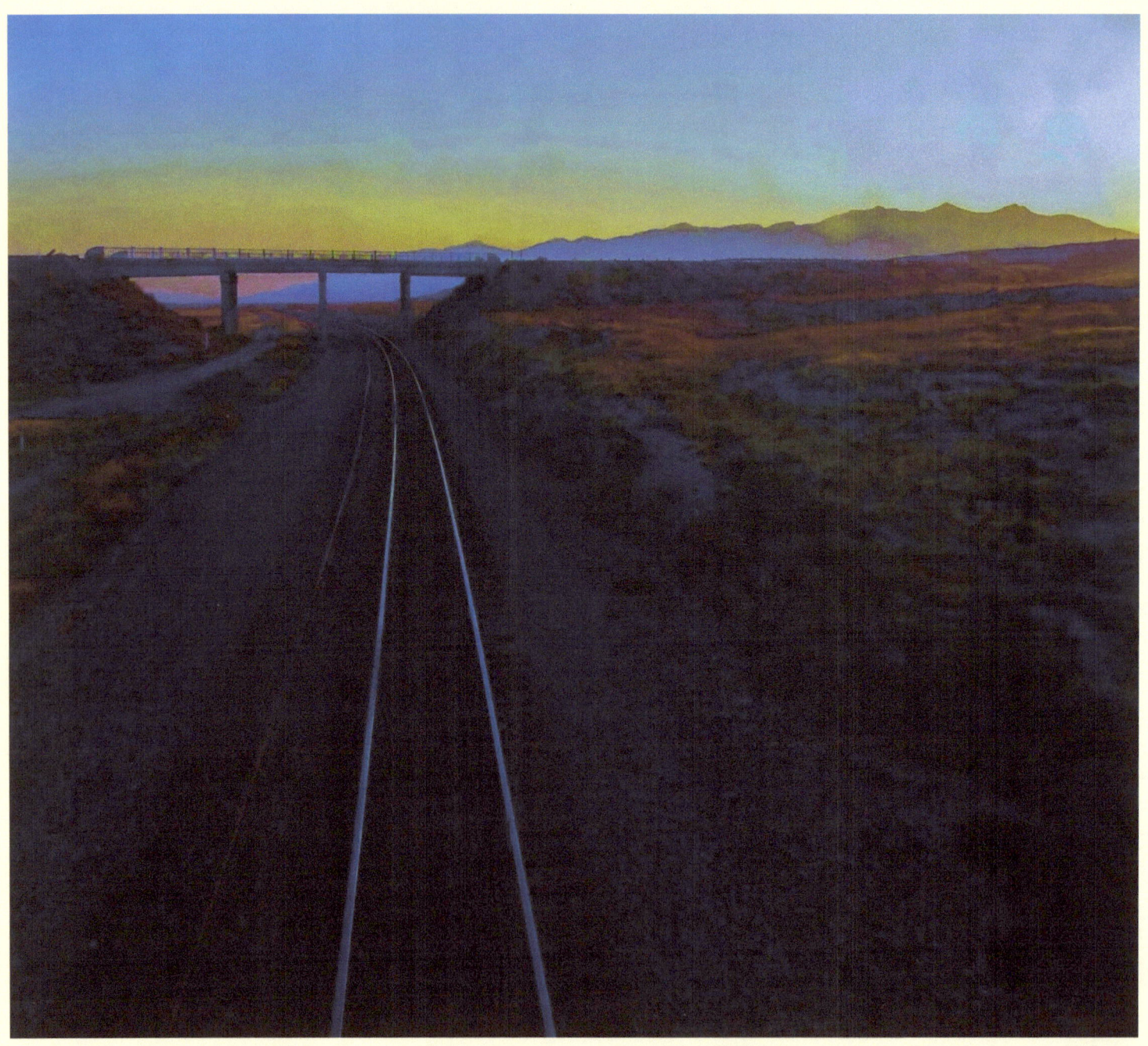

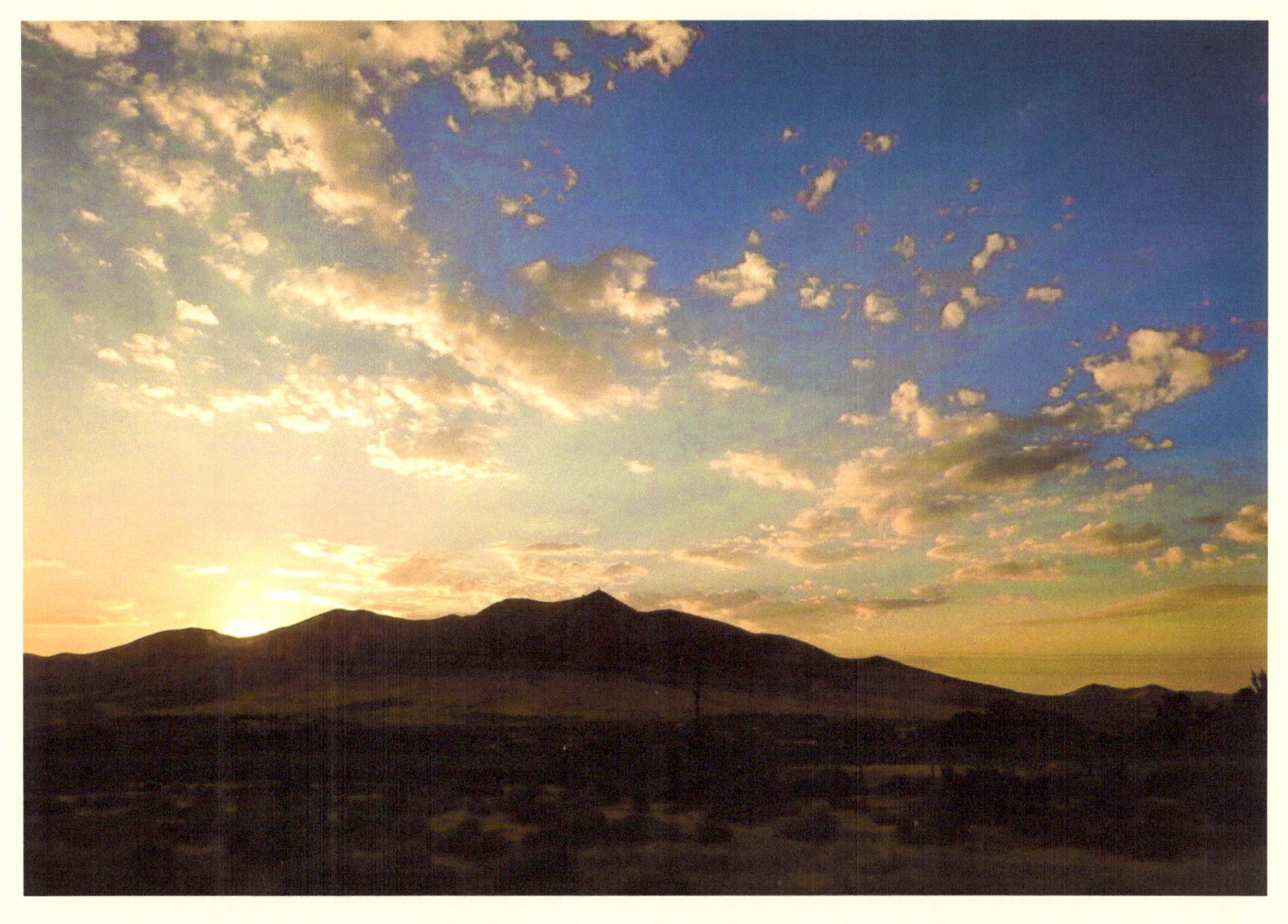

And Nevada's daybreak highlights the

intricacies of its desert floor –

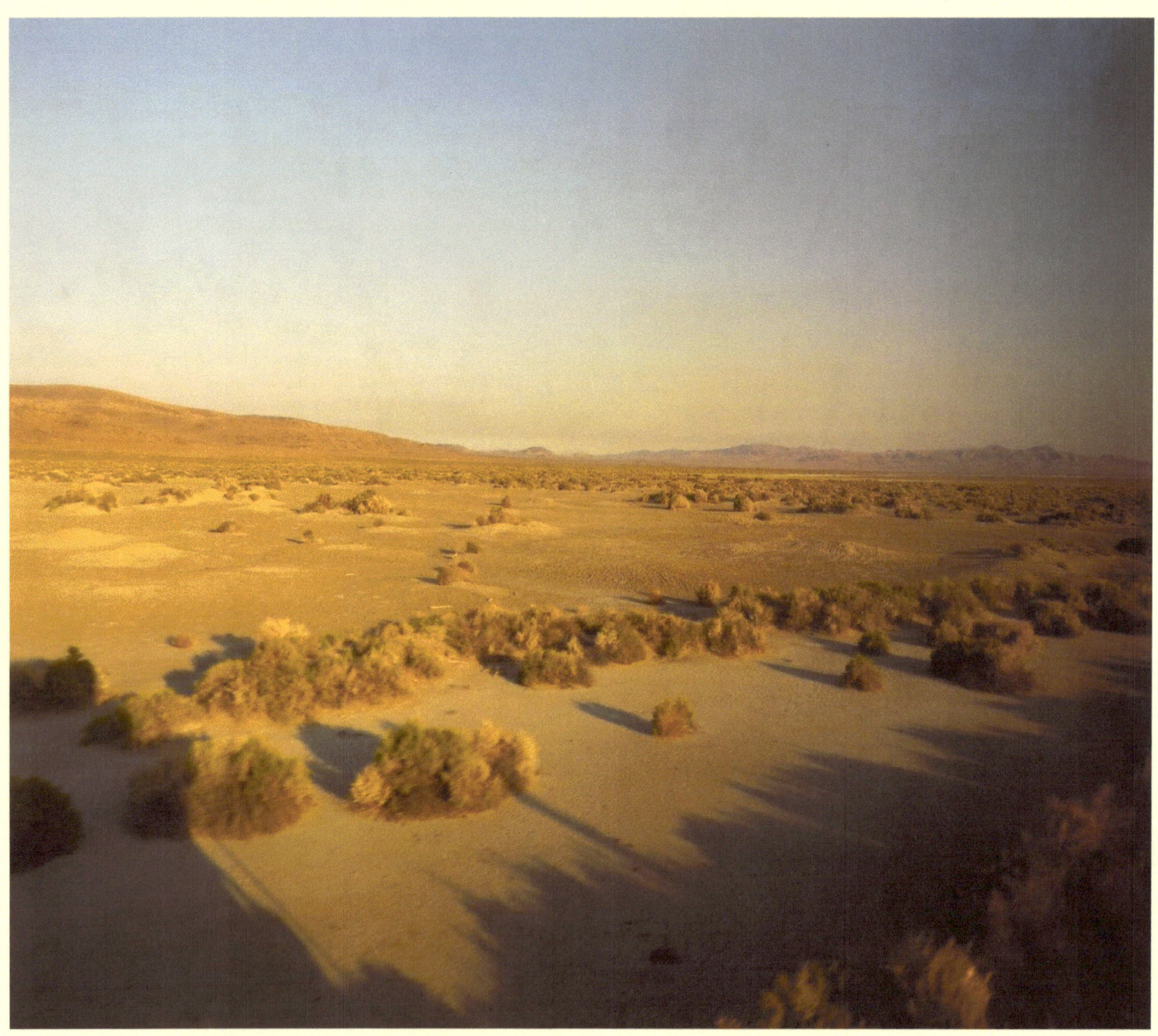

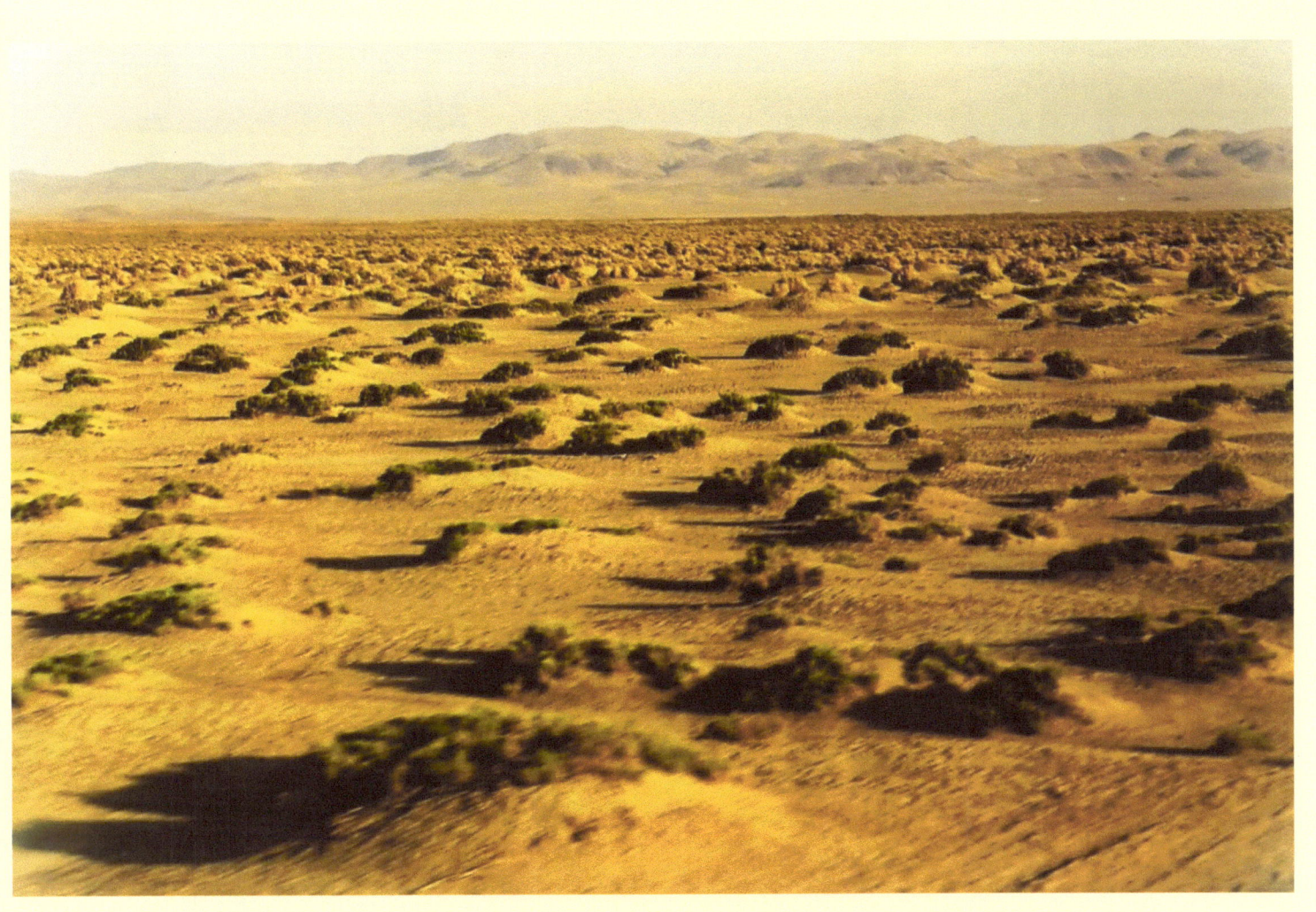

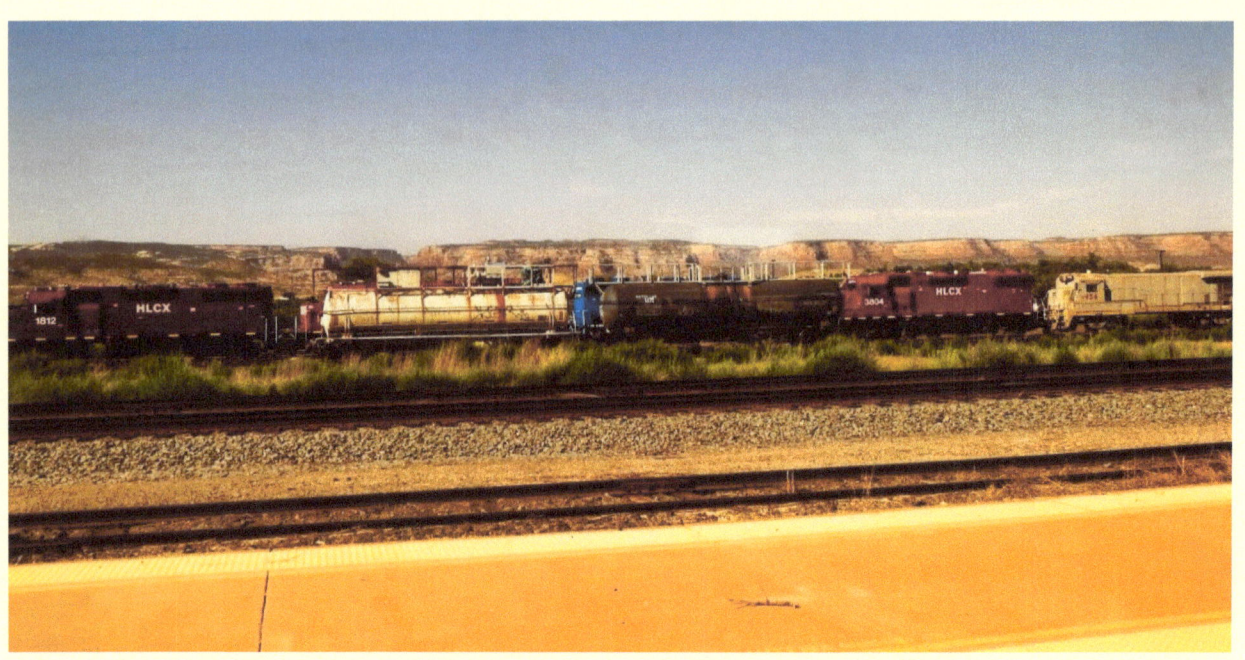

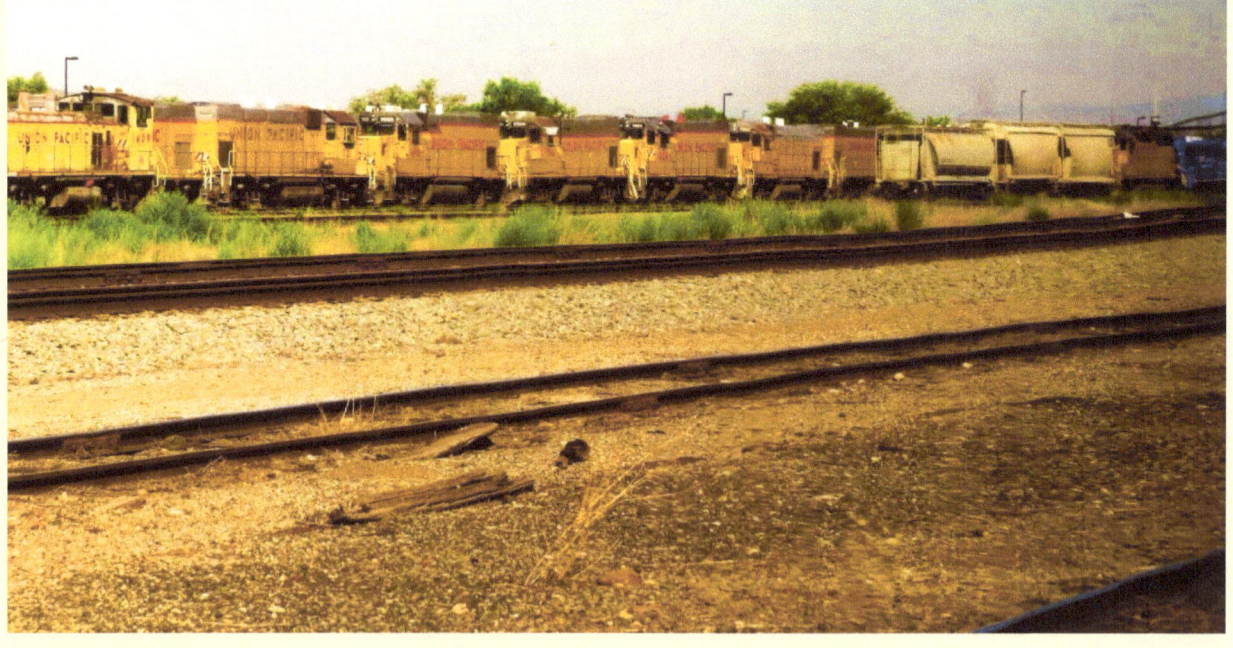

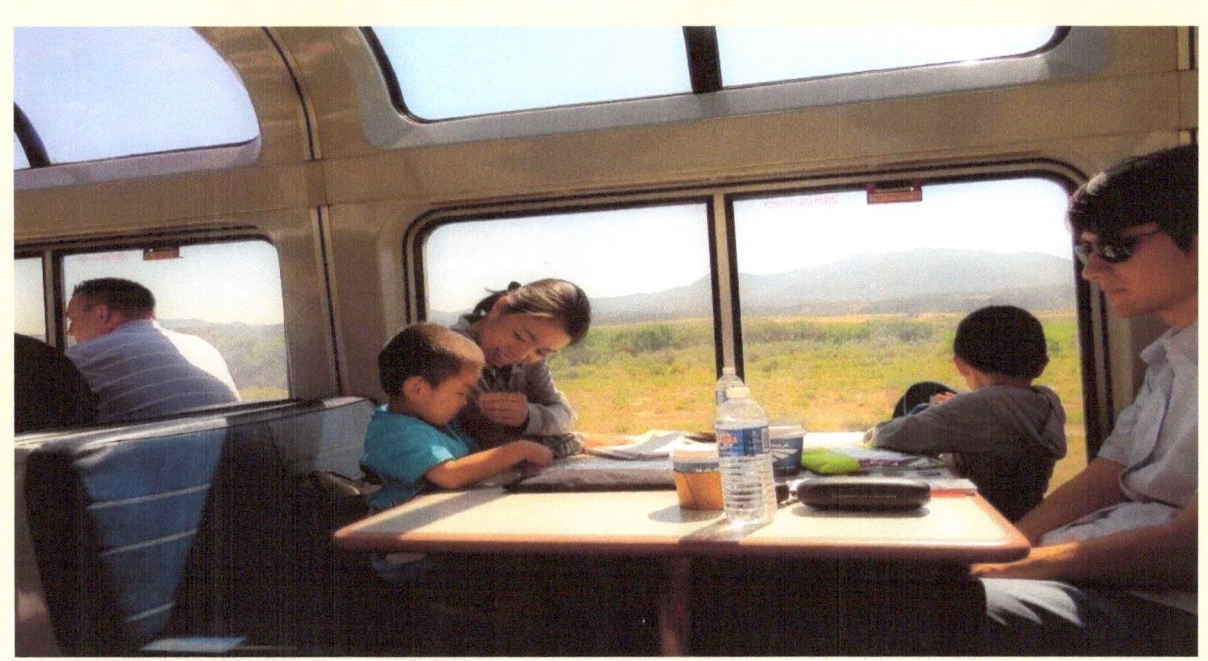
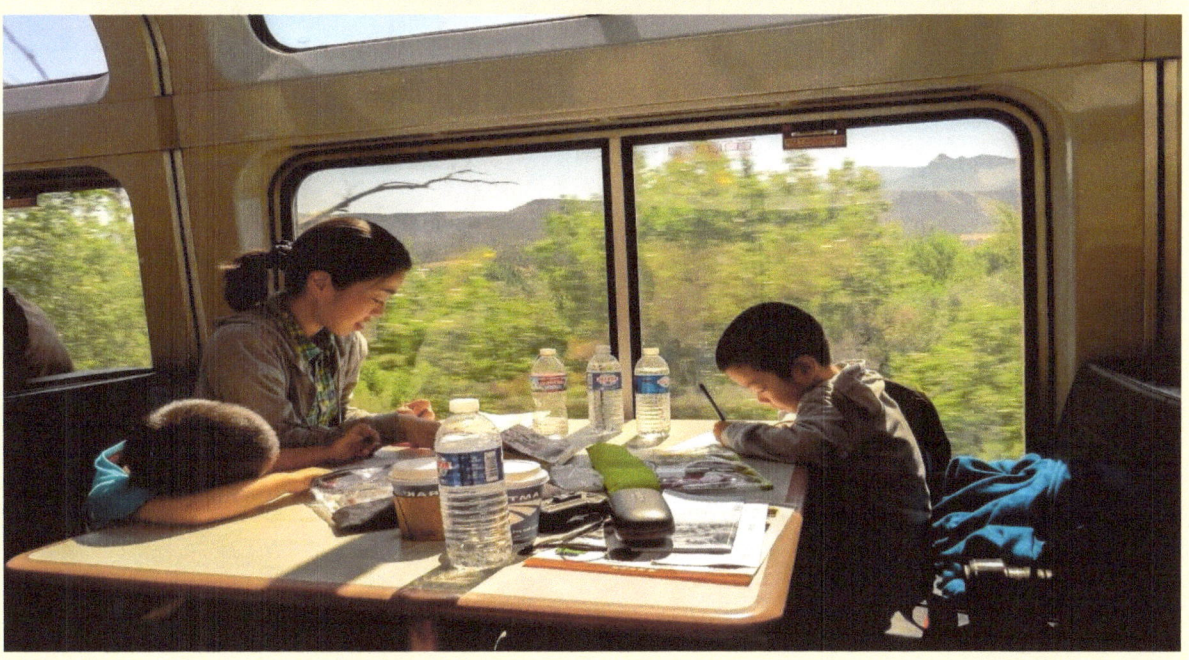

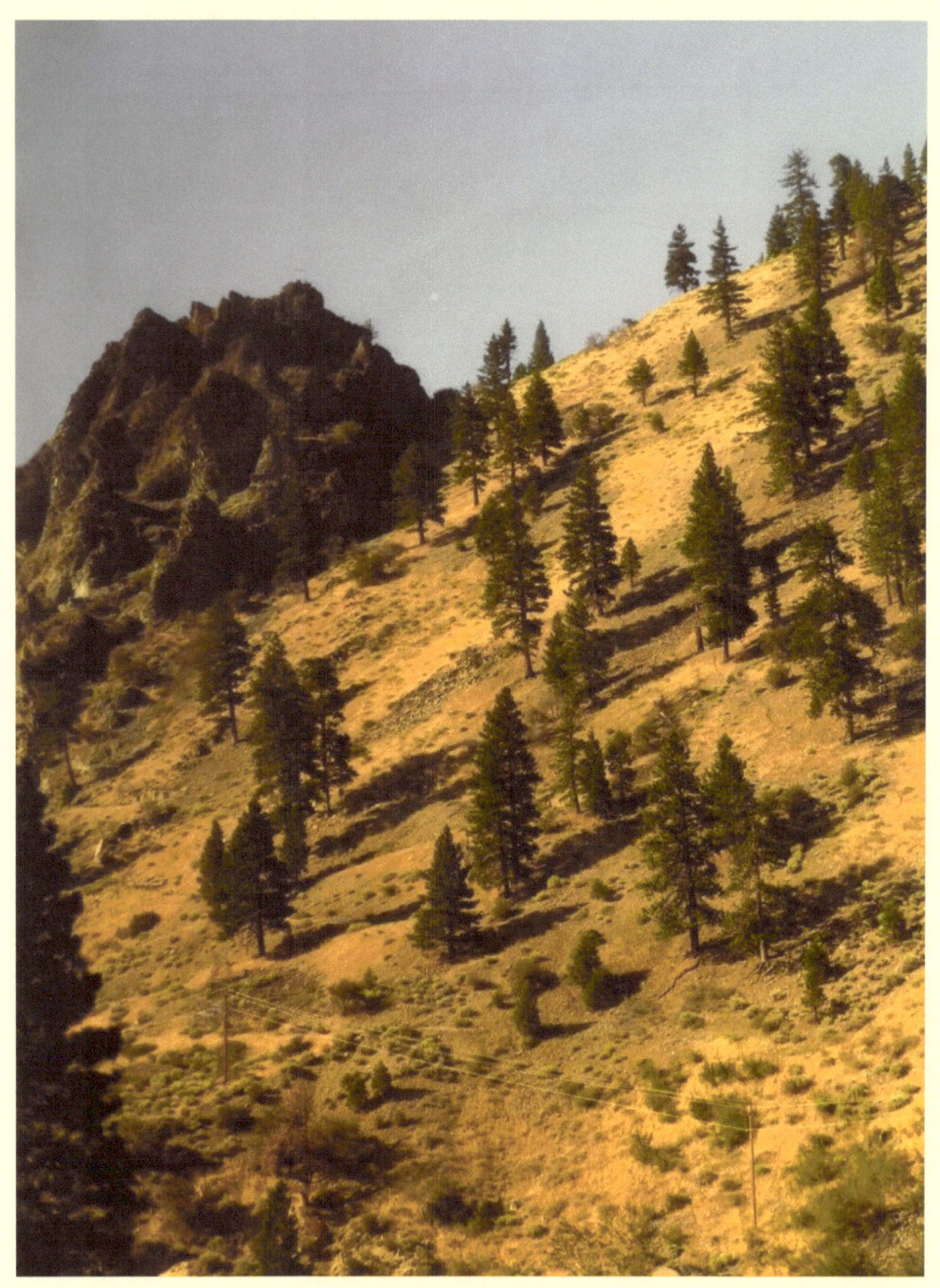

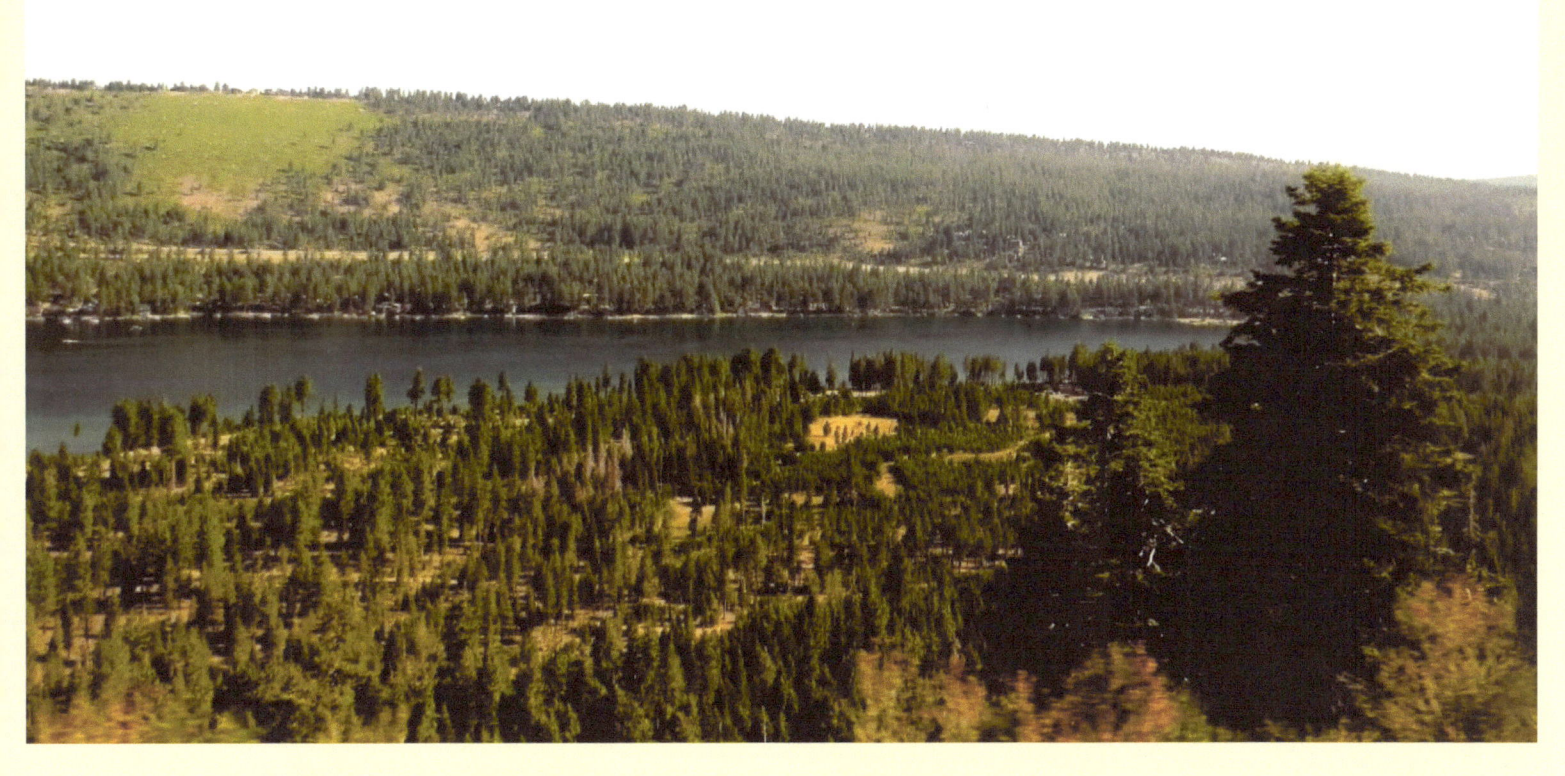

After a climb into the Sierra Nevada mountains,
one glimpses Donner Lake –
near Donner Pass,
where the Donner Party
struggled through that historically wicked Donner winter –

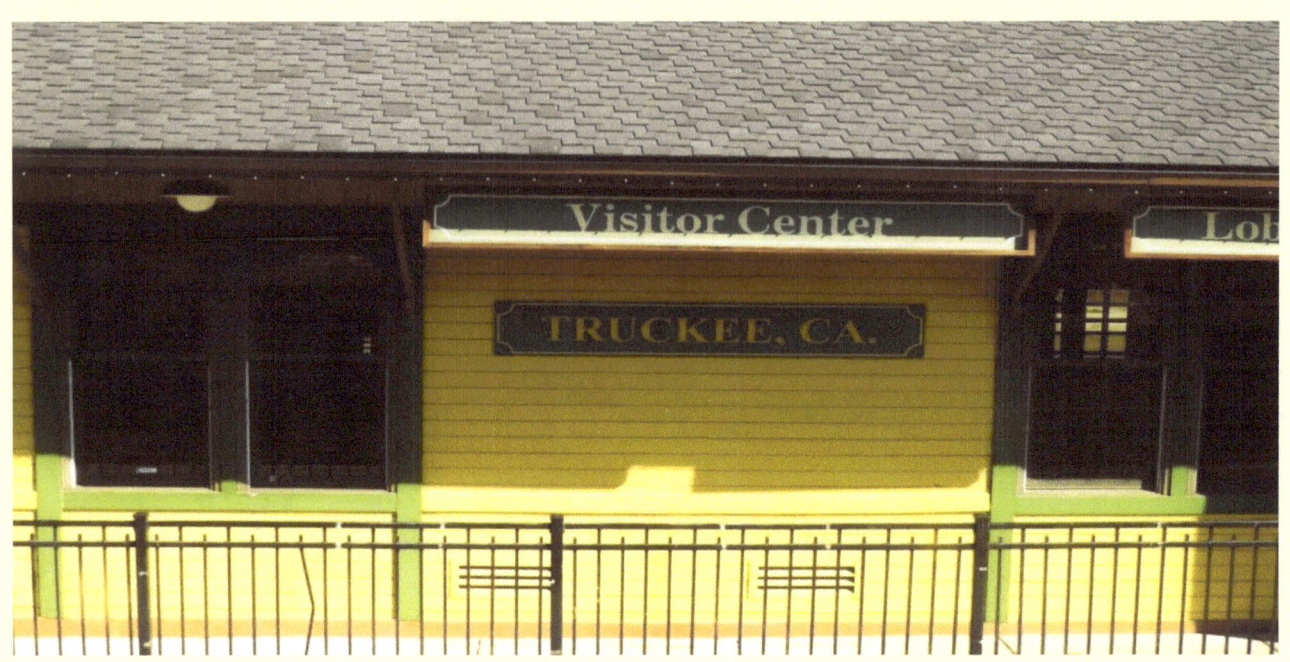

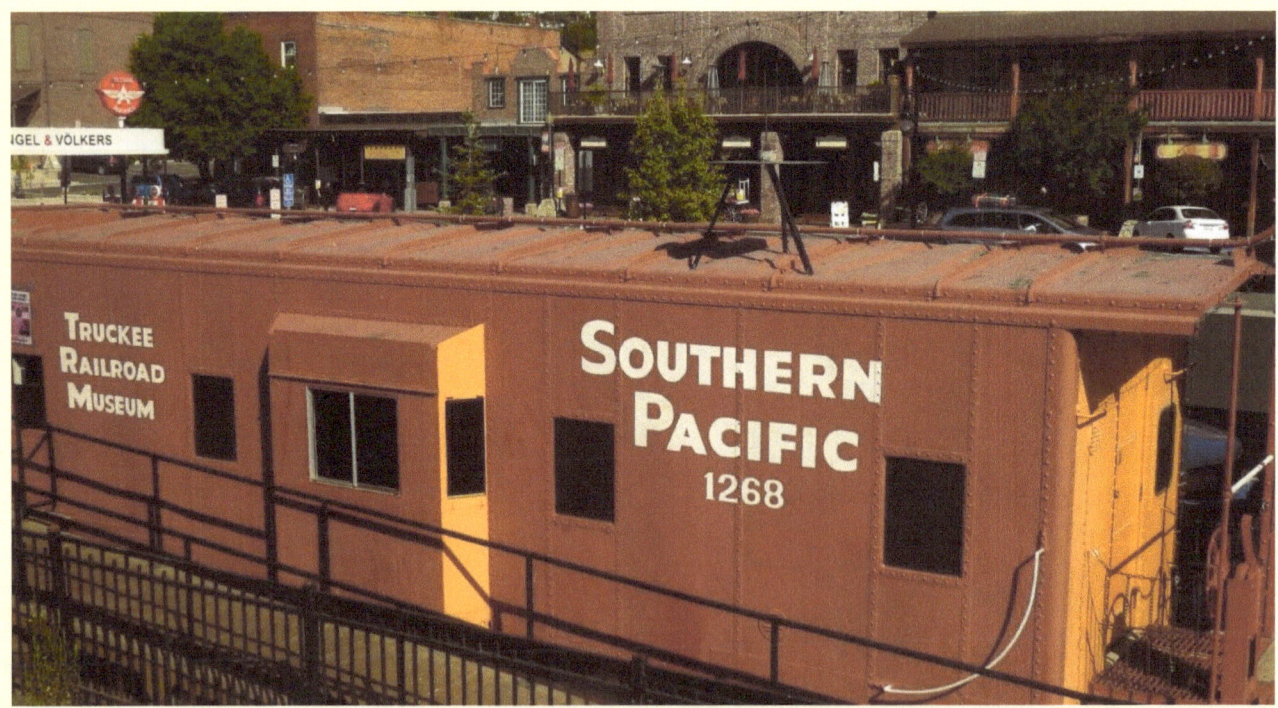

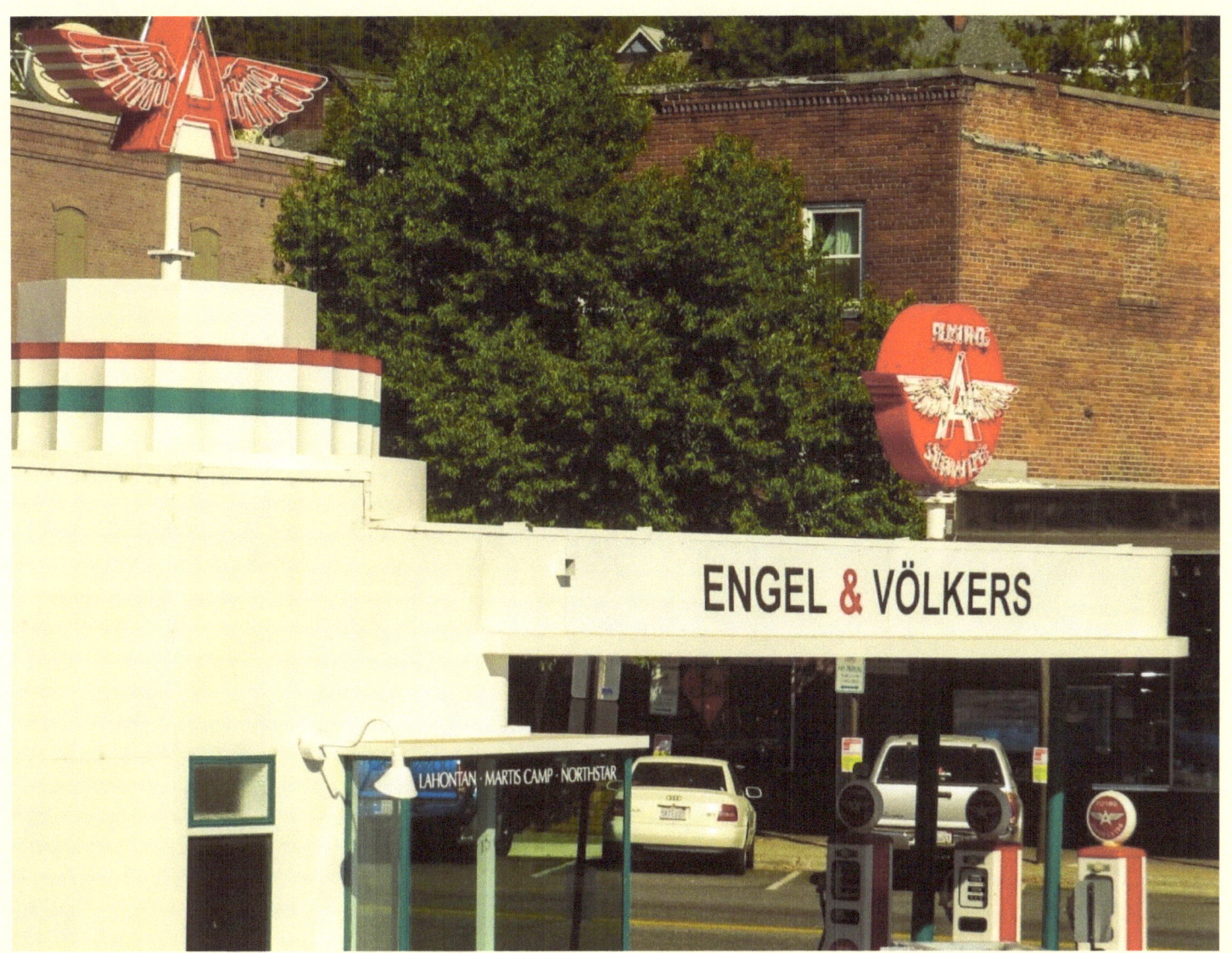

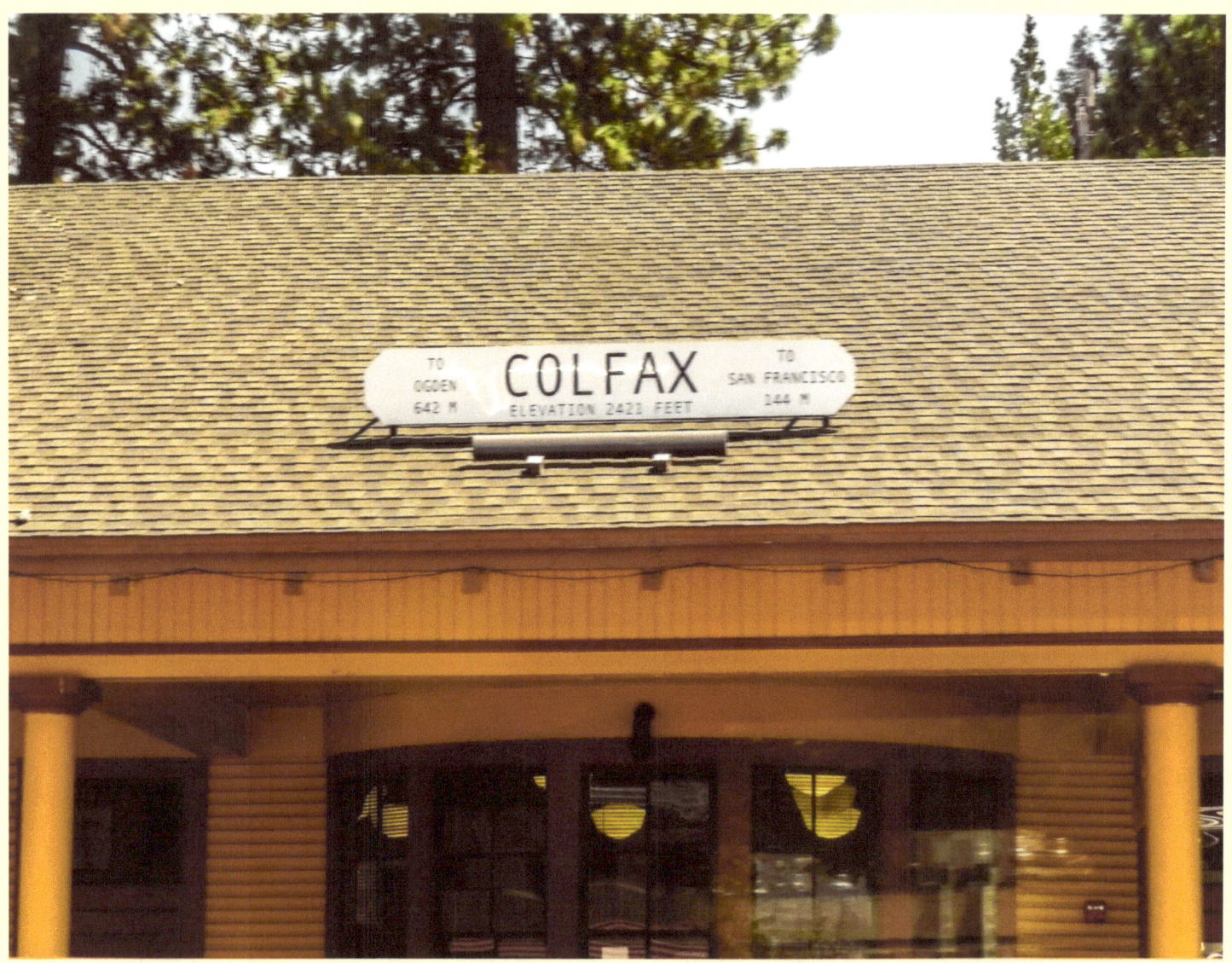

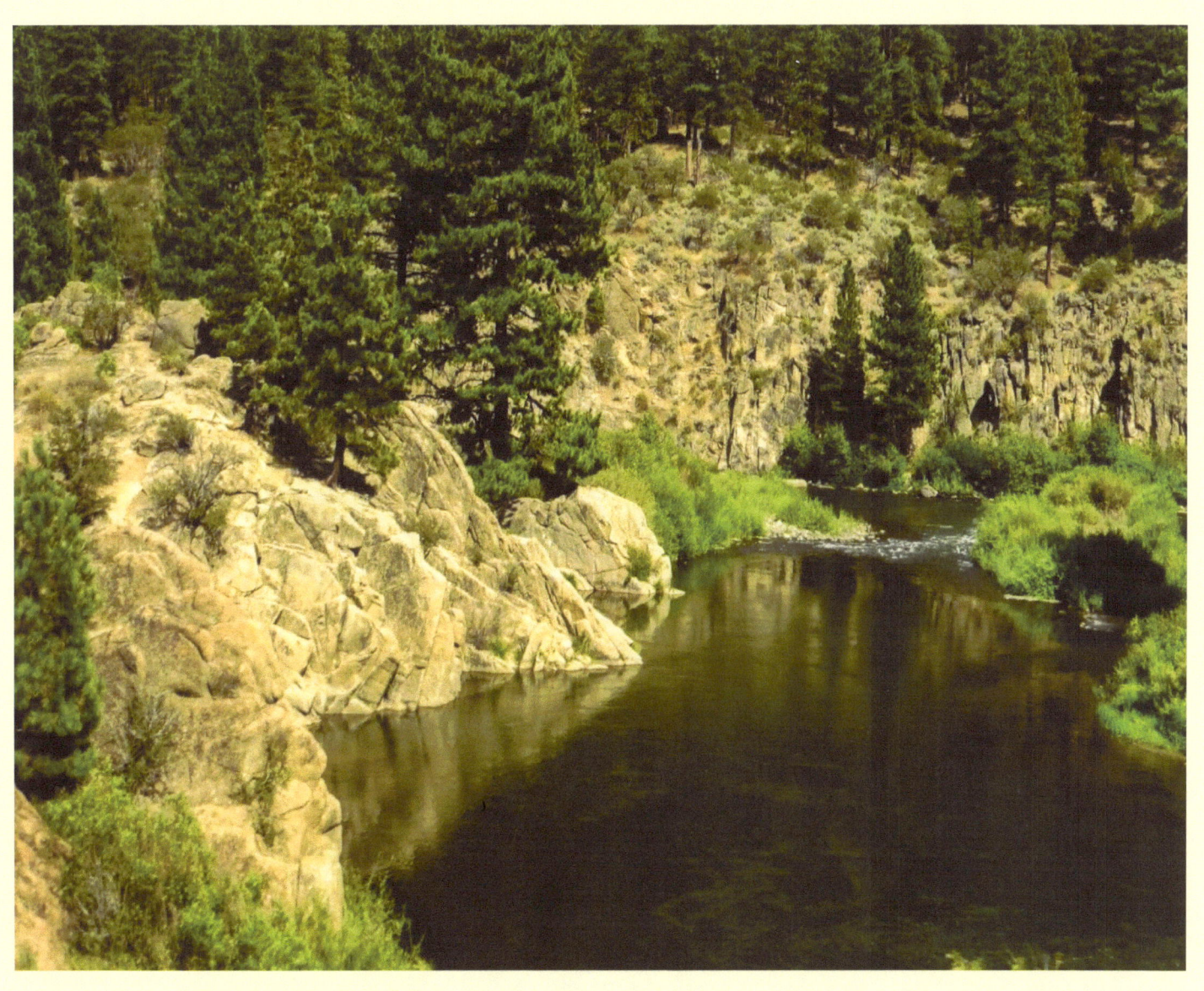

Again, water flowing to the west is harvested –

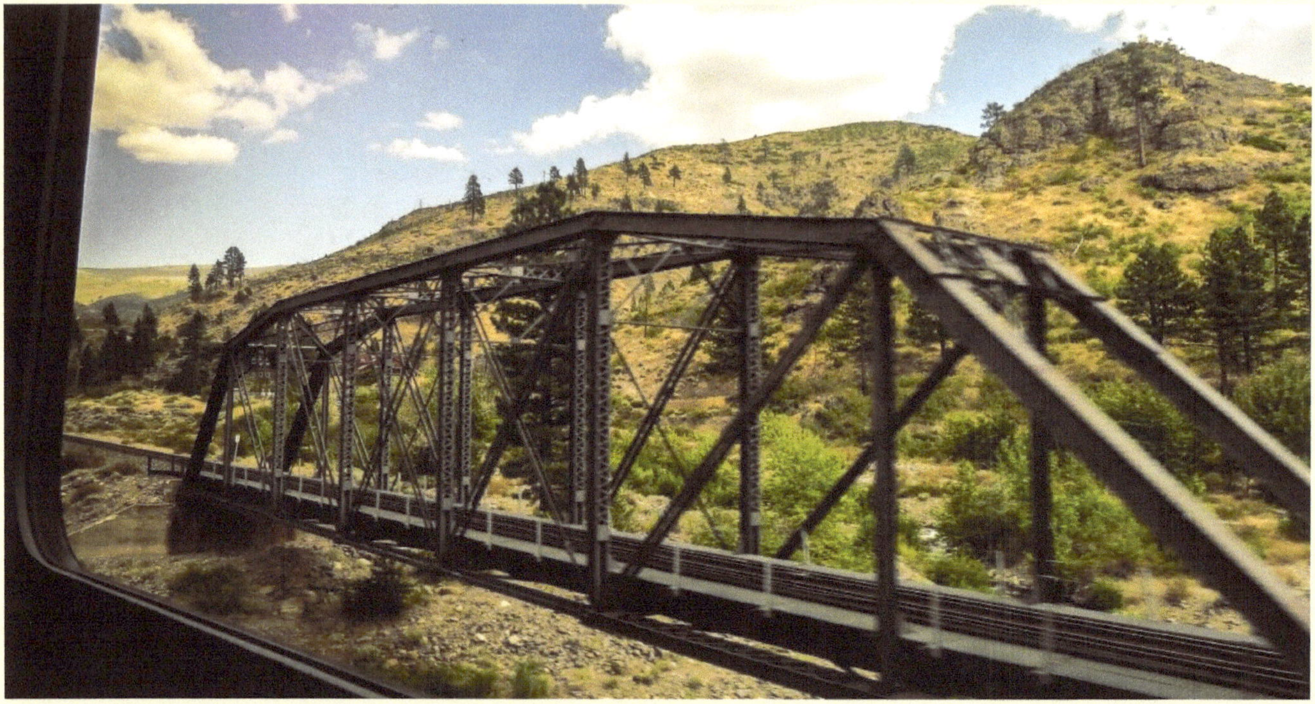

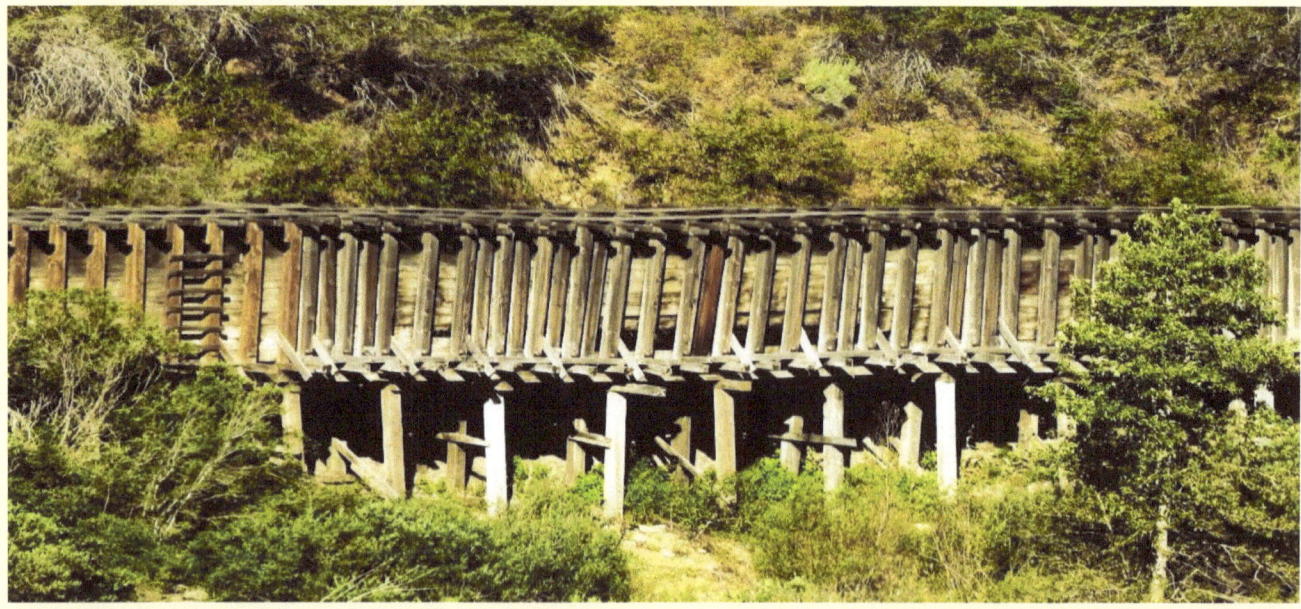

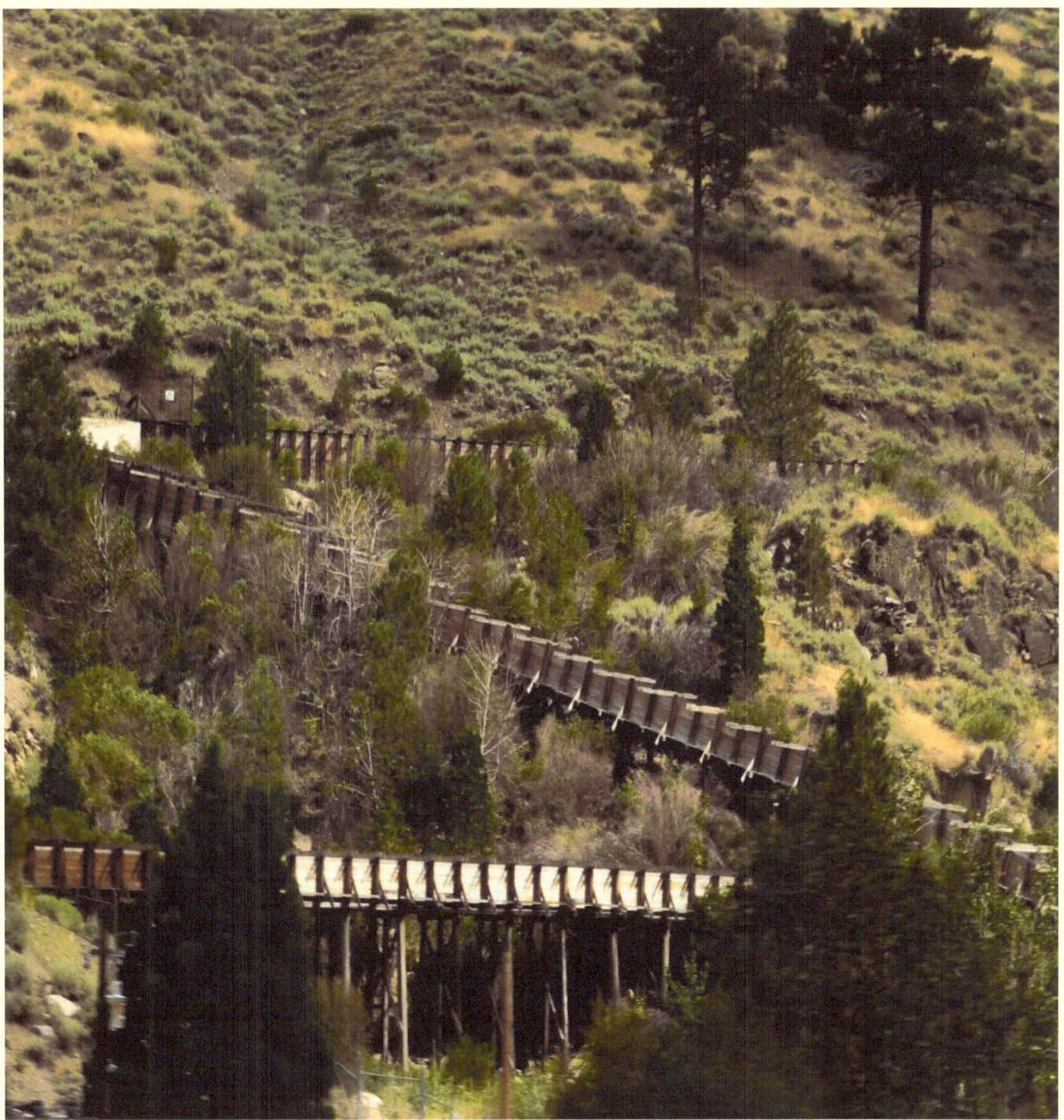

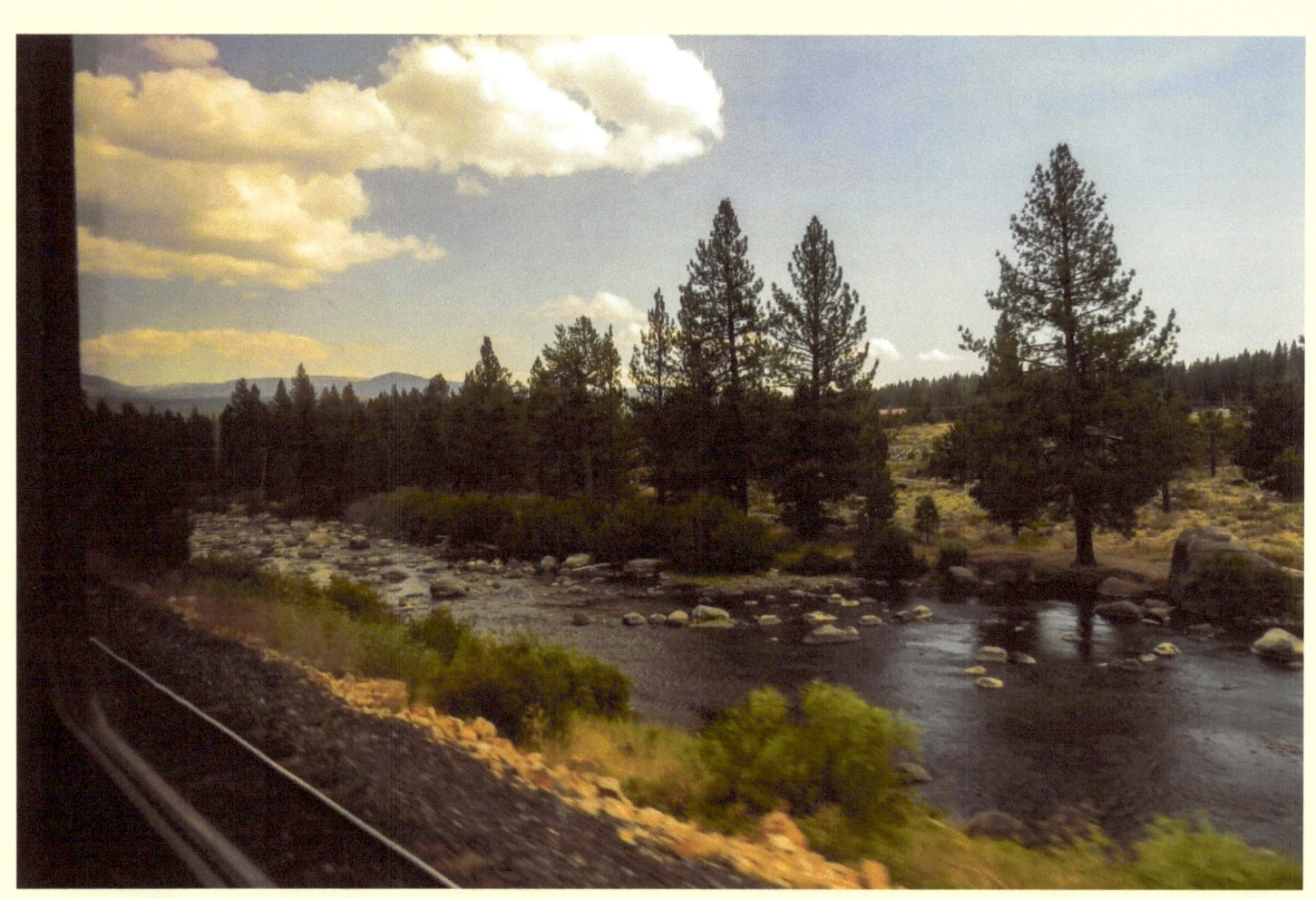

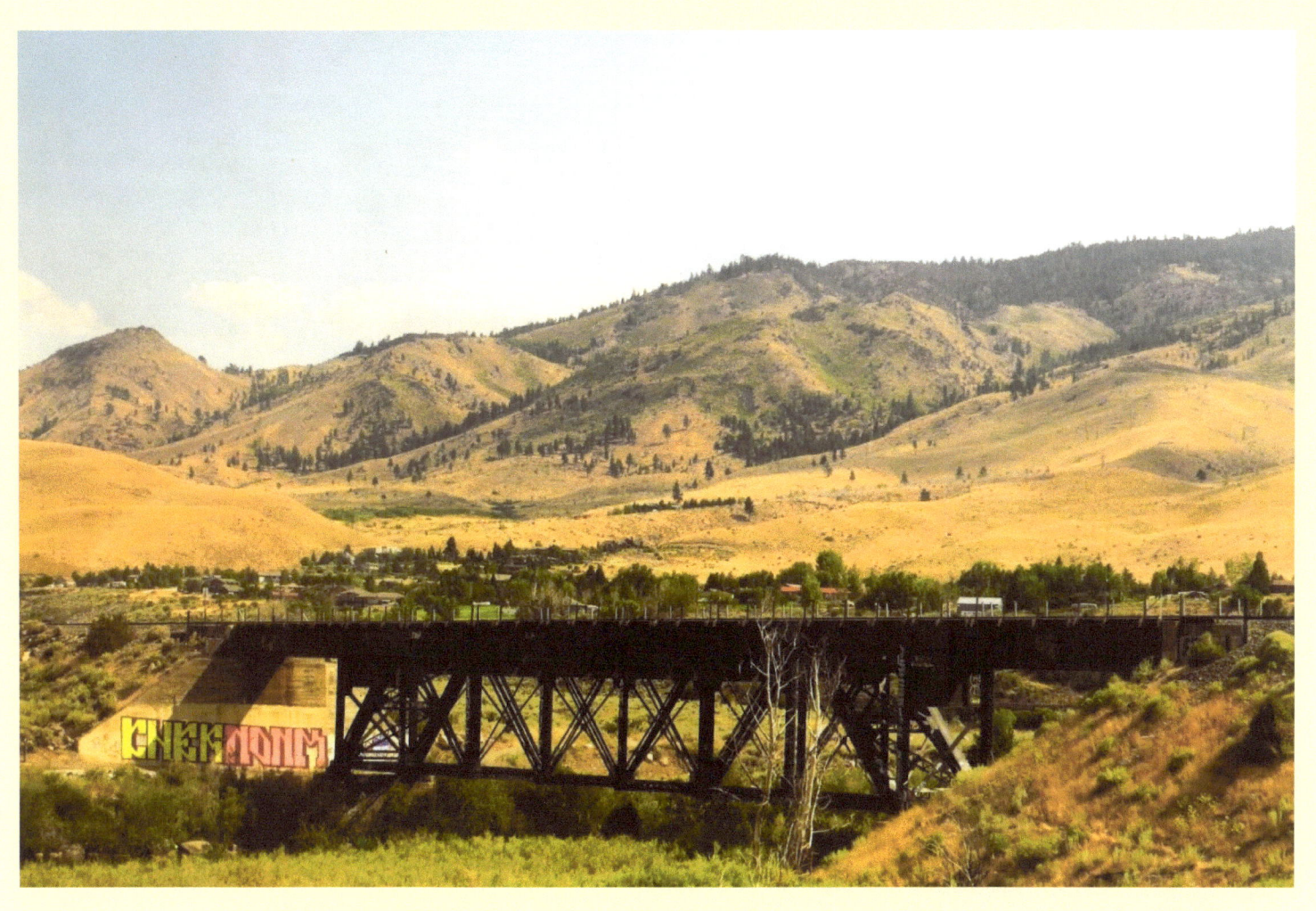

Until the creeks run dry –

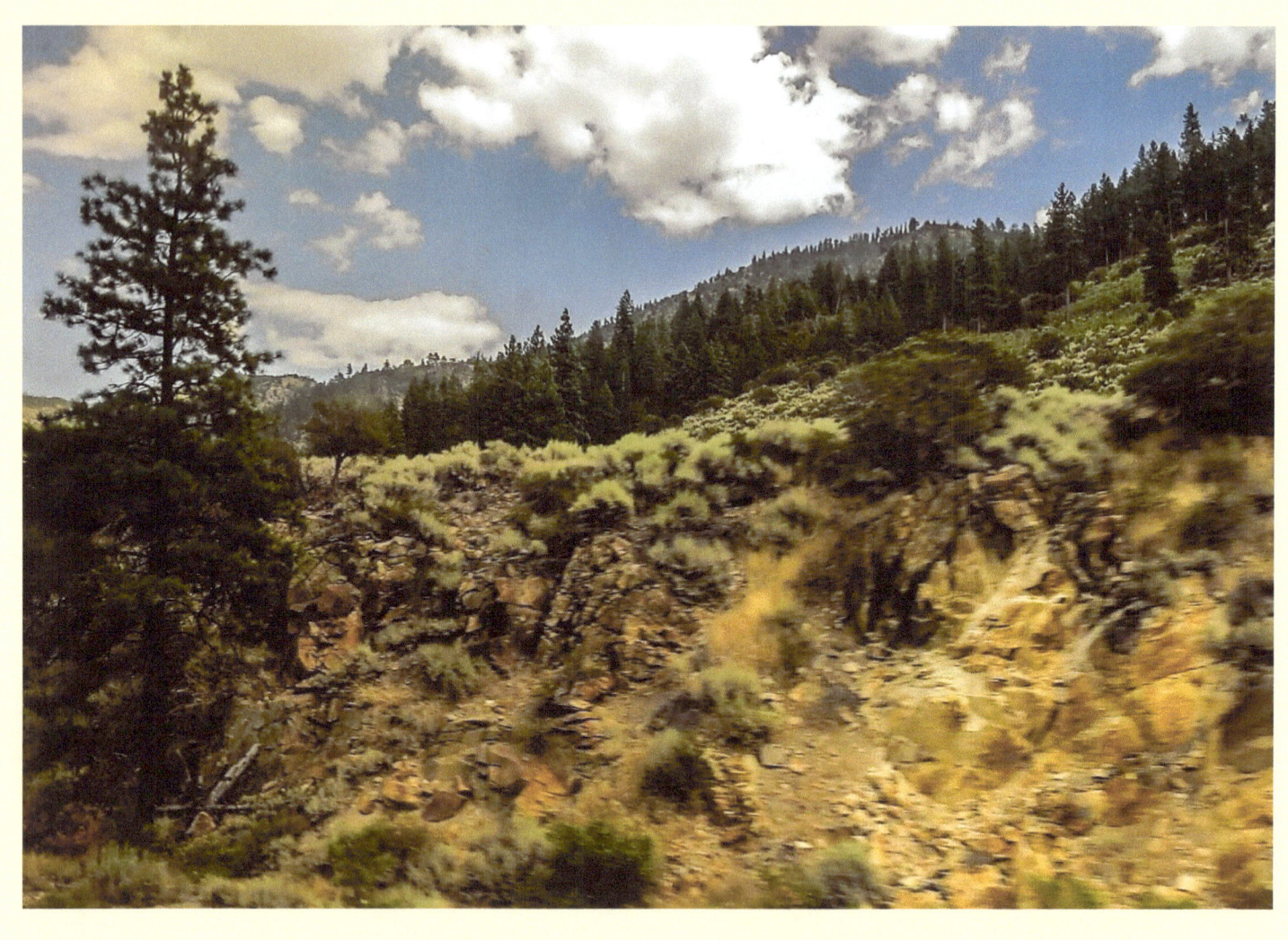

Leaving impressions of simple sagebrush to entertain the eye –

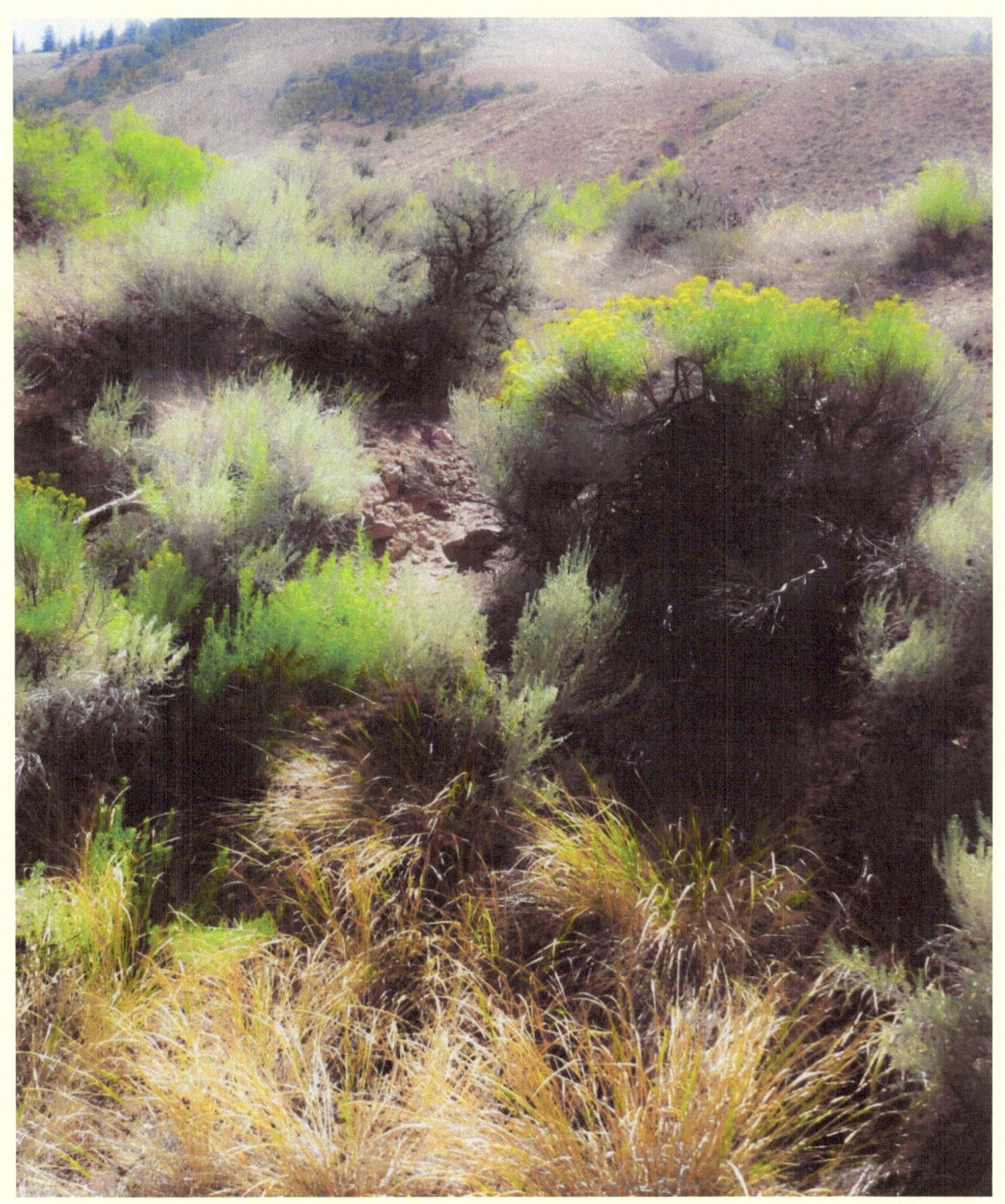

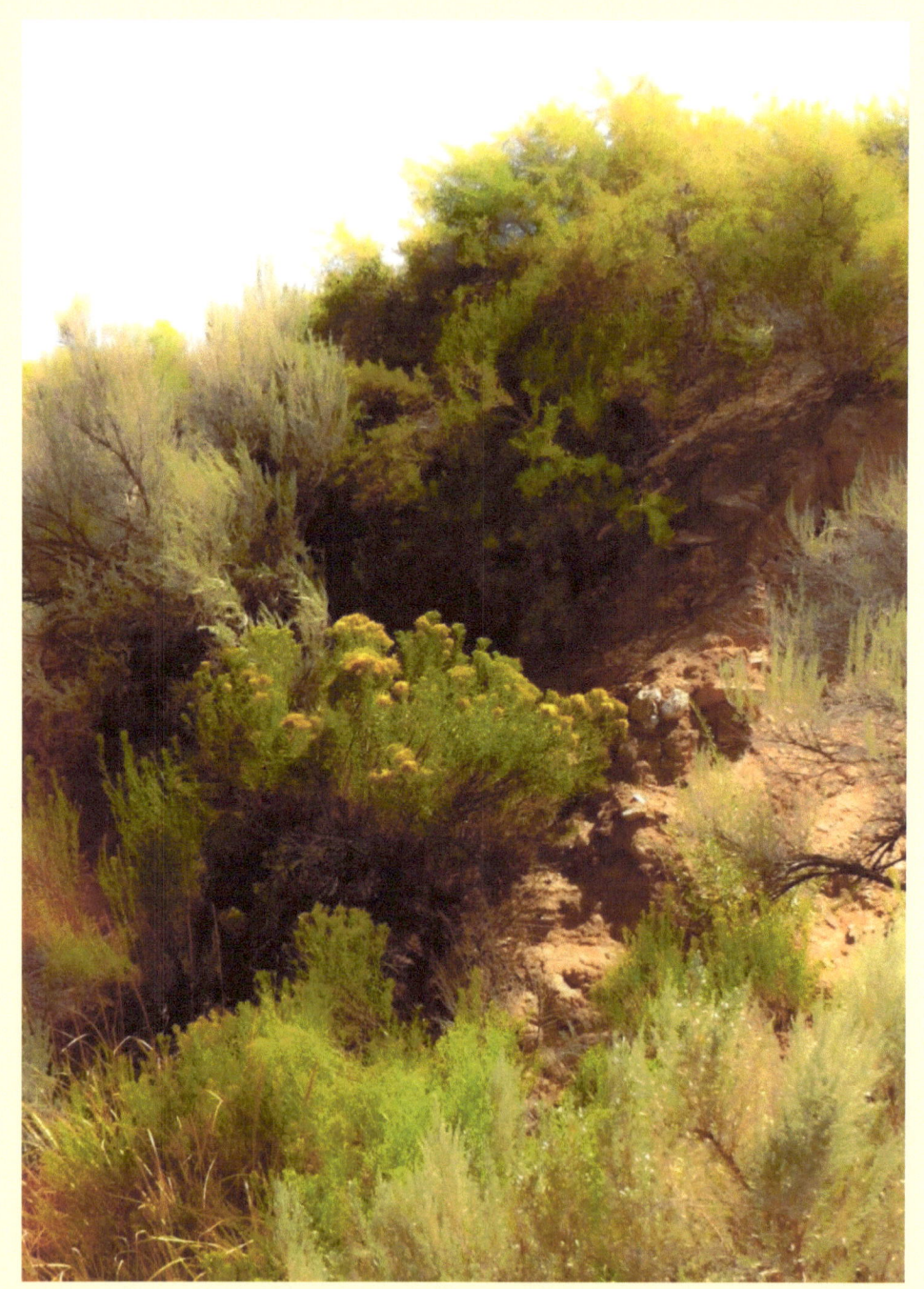

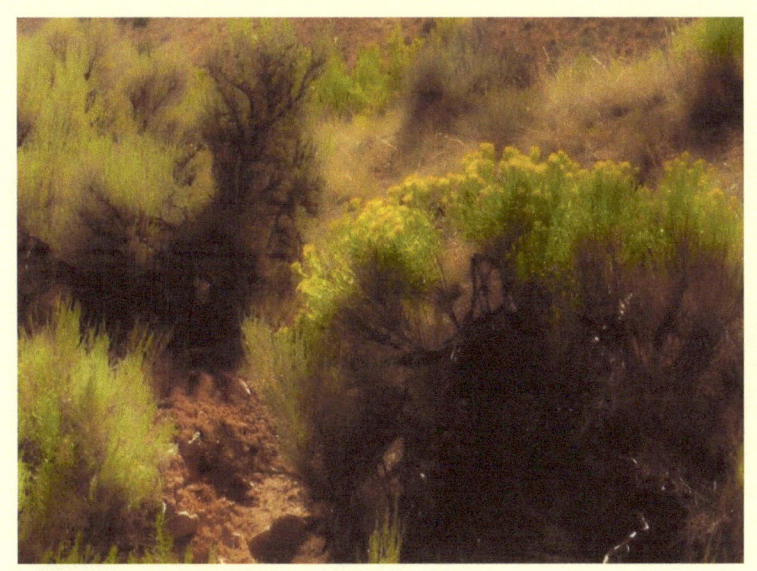
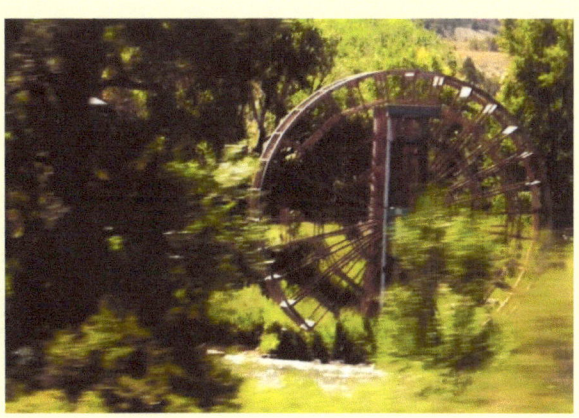

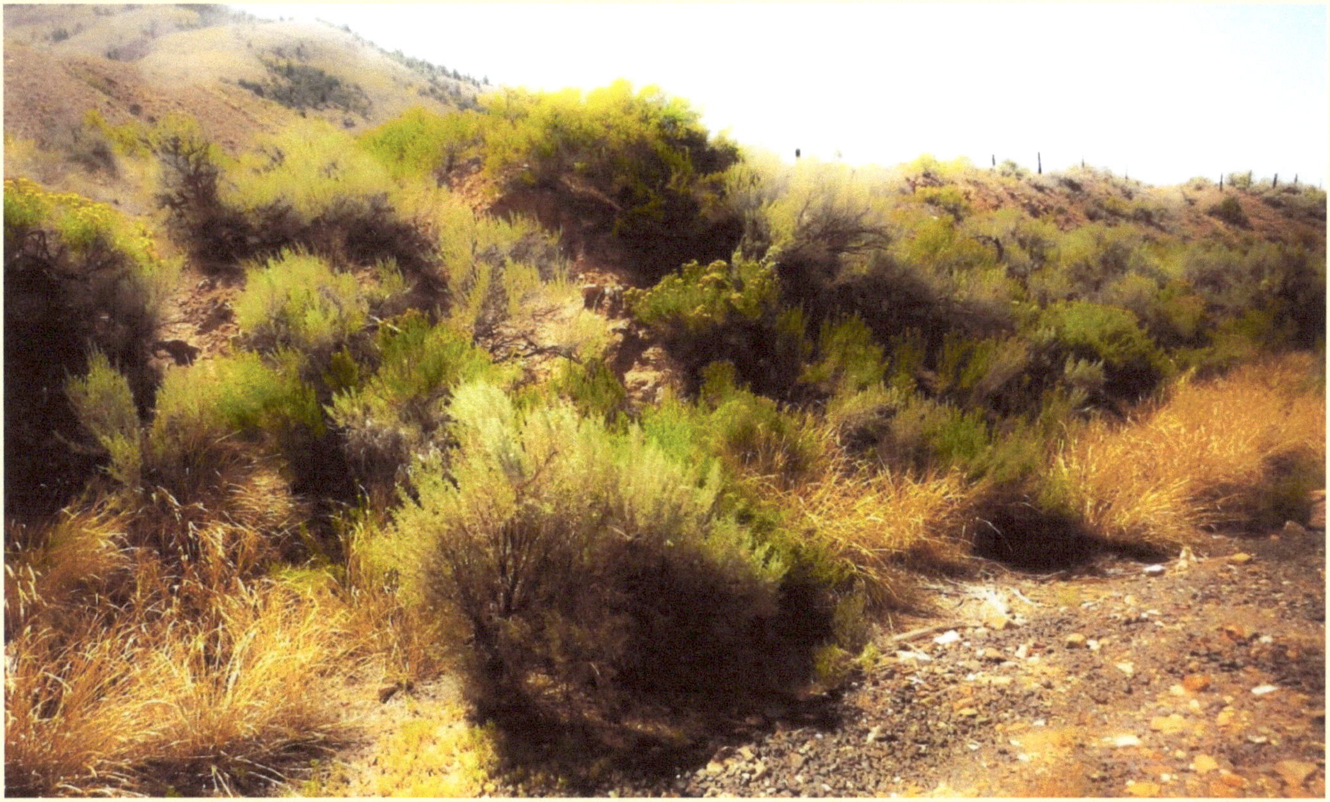

Then, Sacramento blooms, a pale rose in the desert –

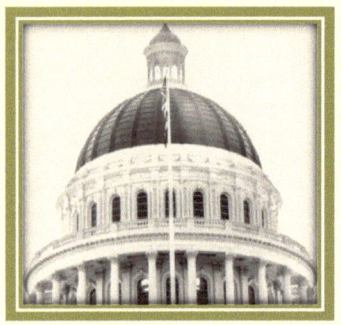

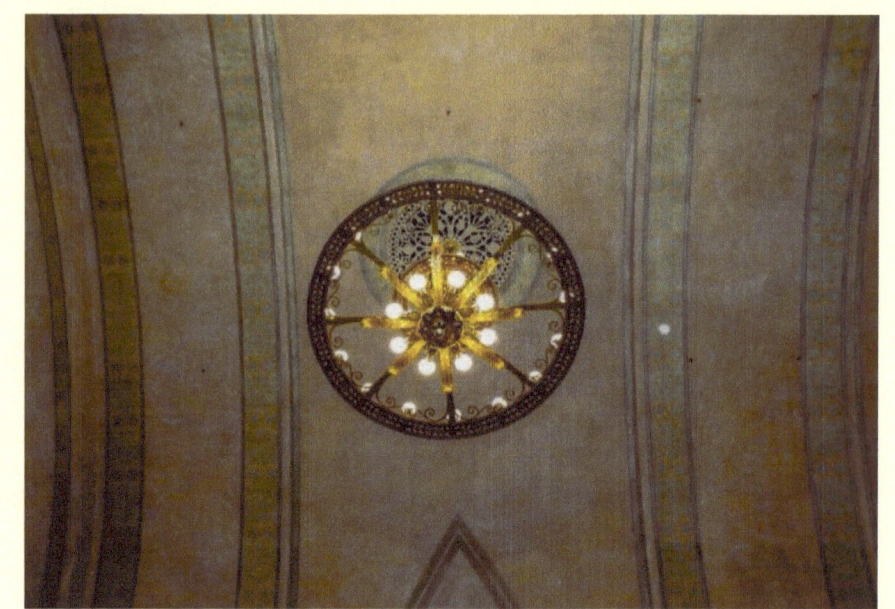

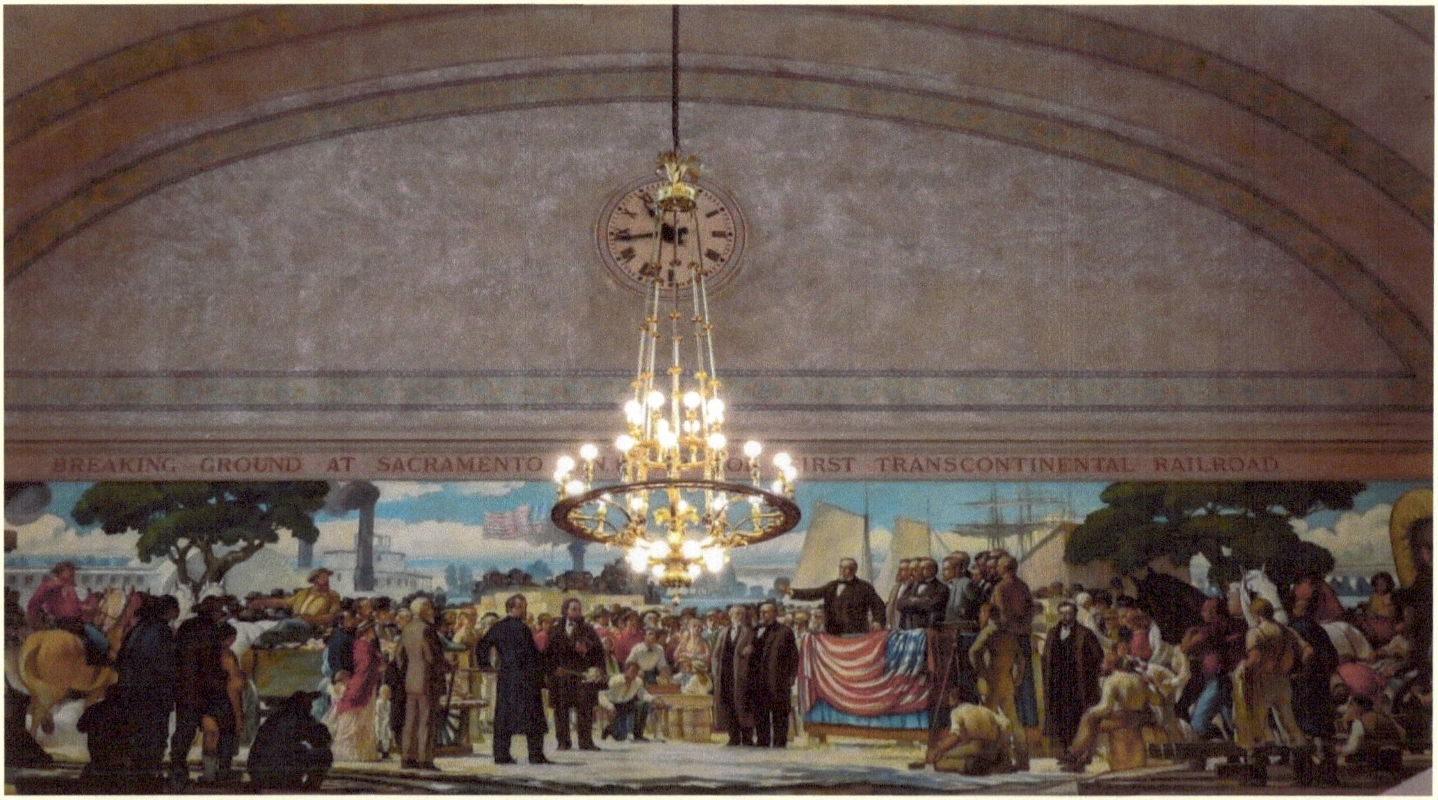

BREAKING GROUND AT SACRAMENTO ... FIRST TRANSCONTINENTAL RAILROAD

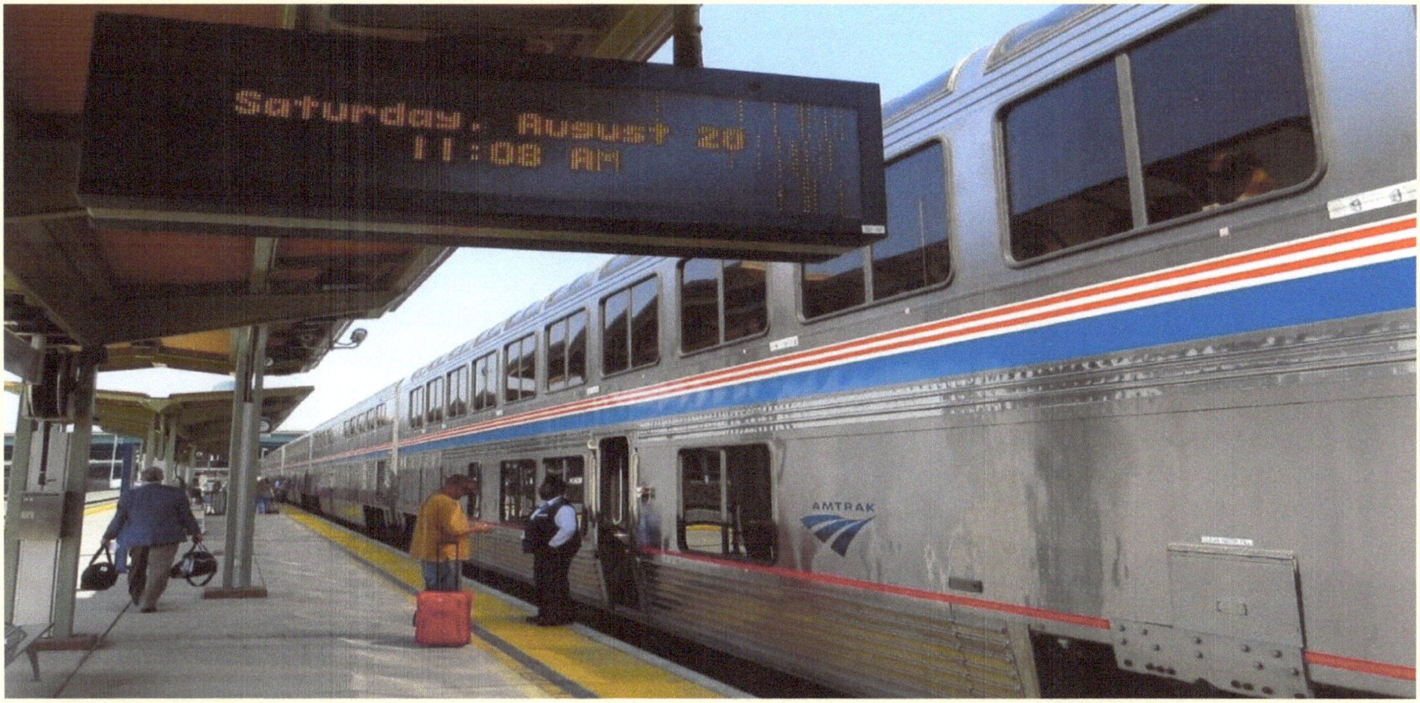
Saturday, August 20
11:08 AM
AMTRAK

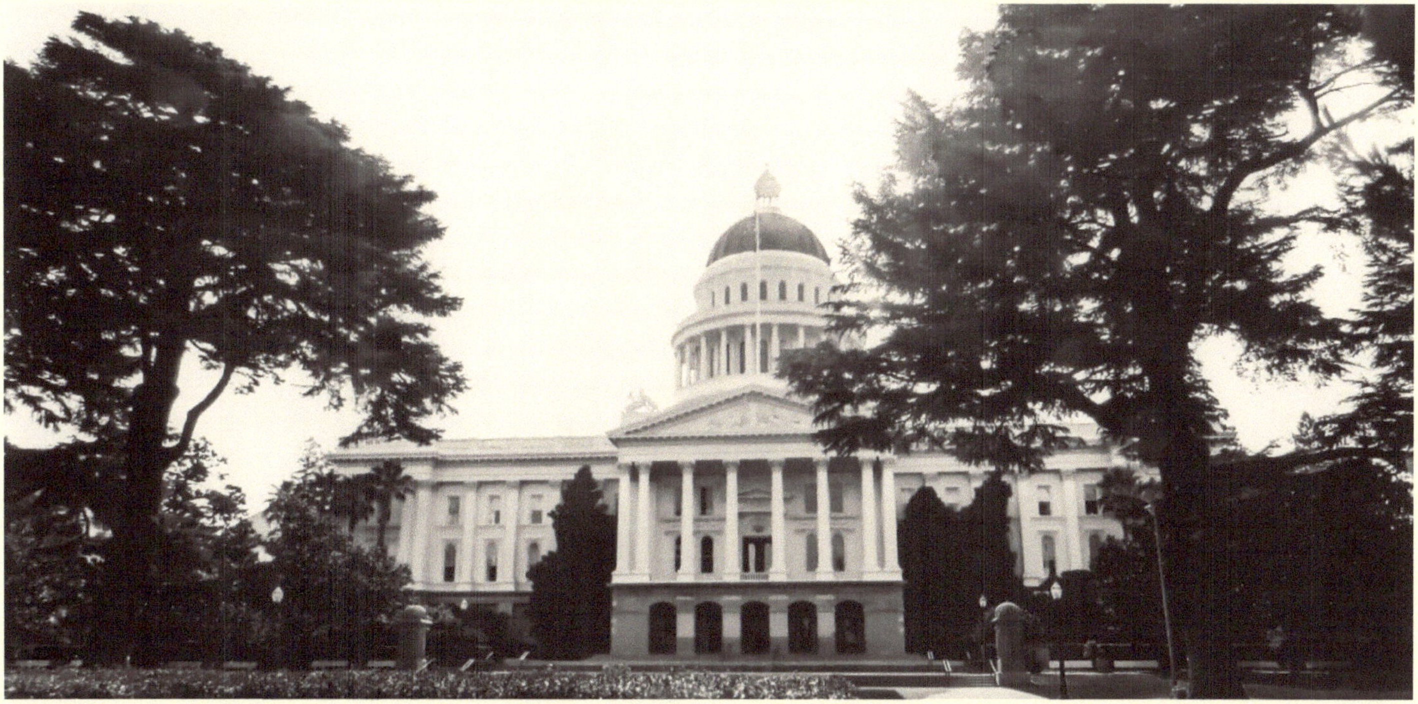

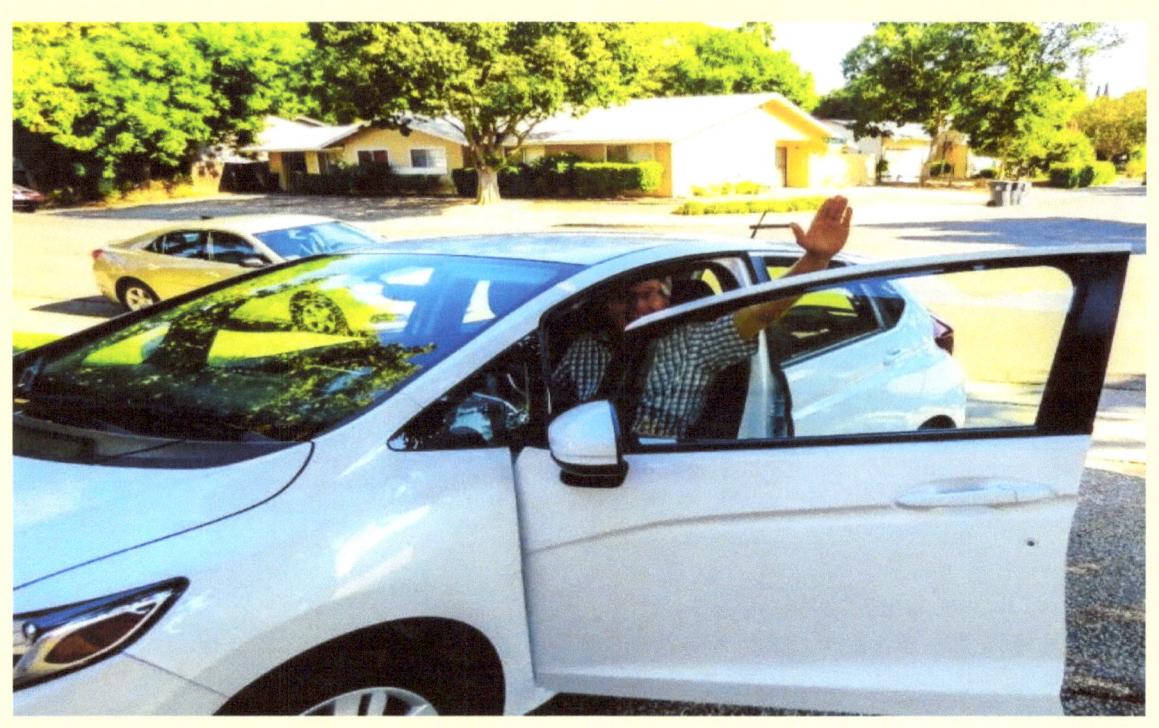

And locals
celebrate the
discovery of
of a shady parking
space –

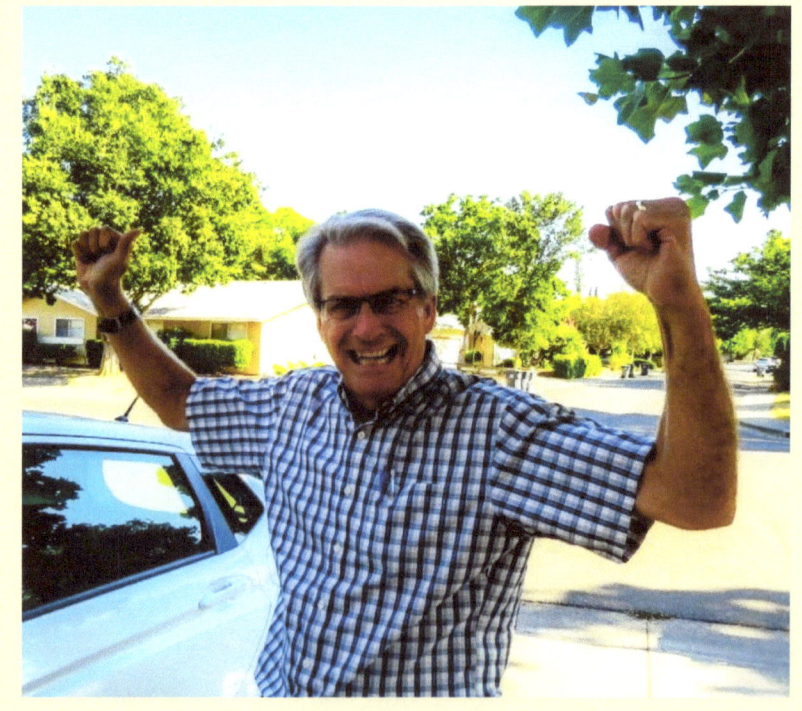

Now, to follow the San Joaquin valley –
south, between rows of pistachios
and newly planted figs –

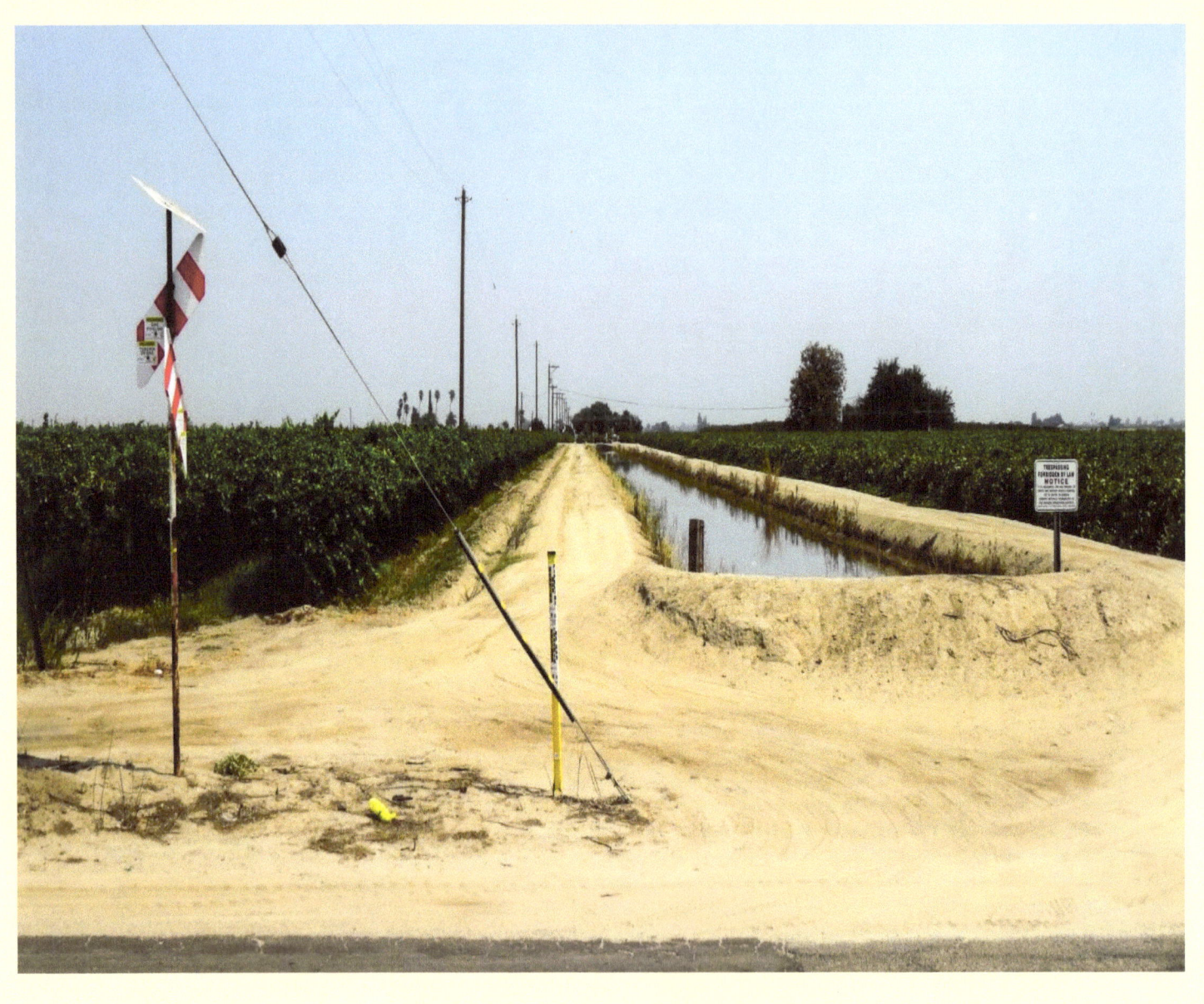

Through irrigated fields –

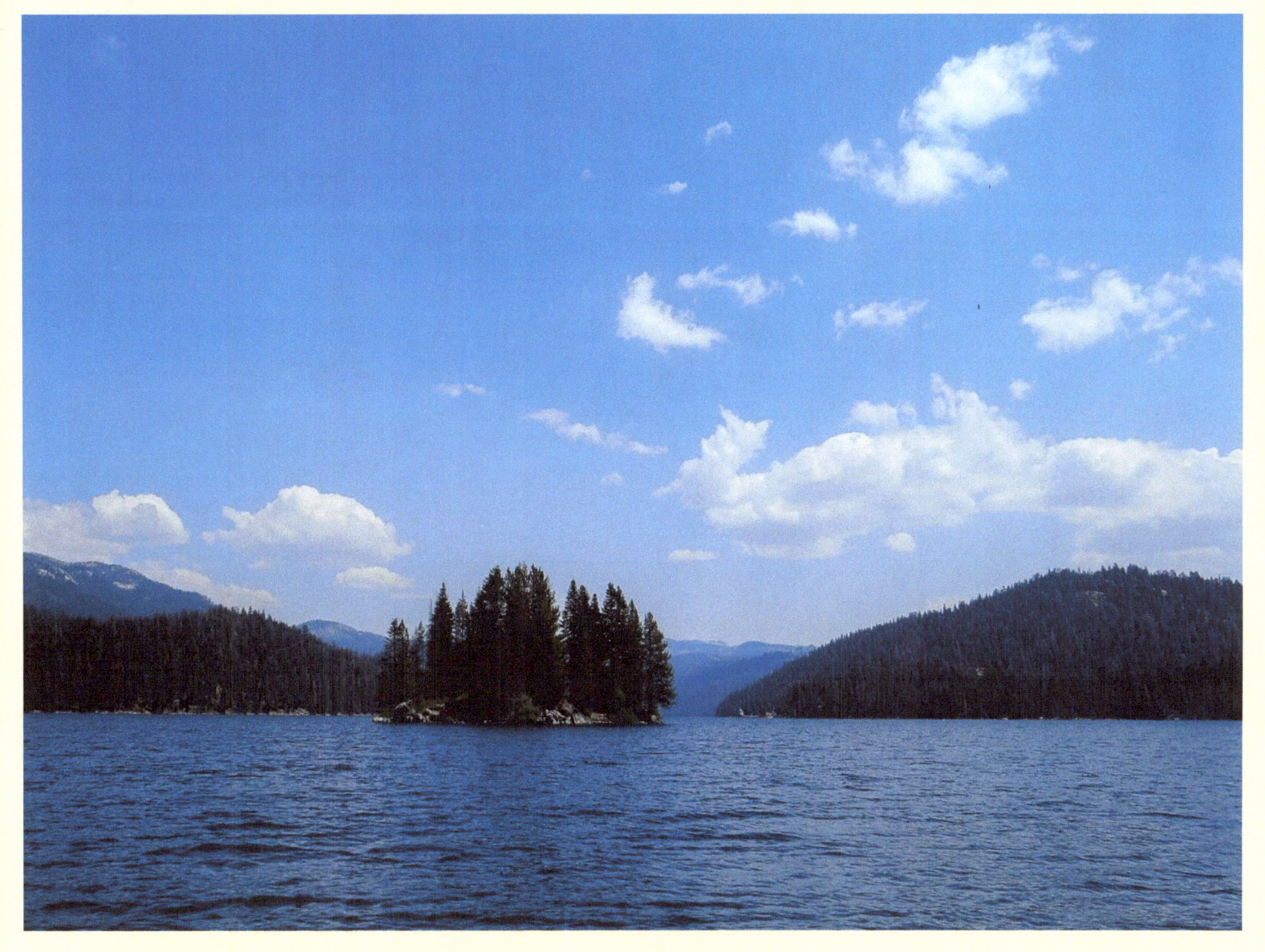

To a perfect lake tucked high in the mountains –

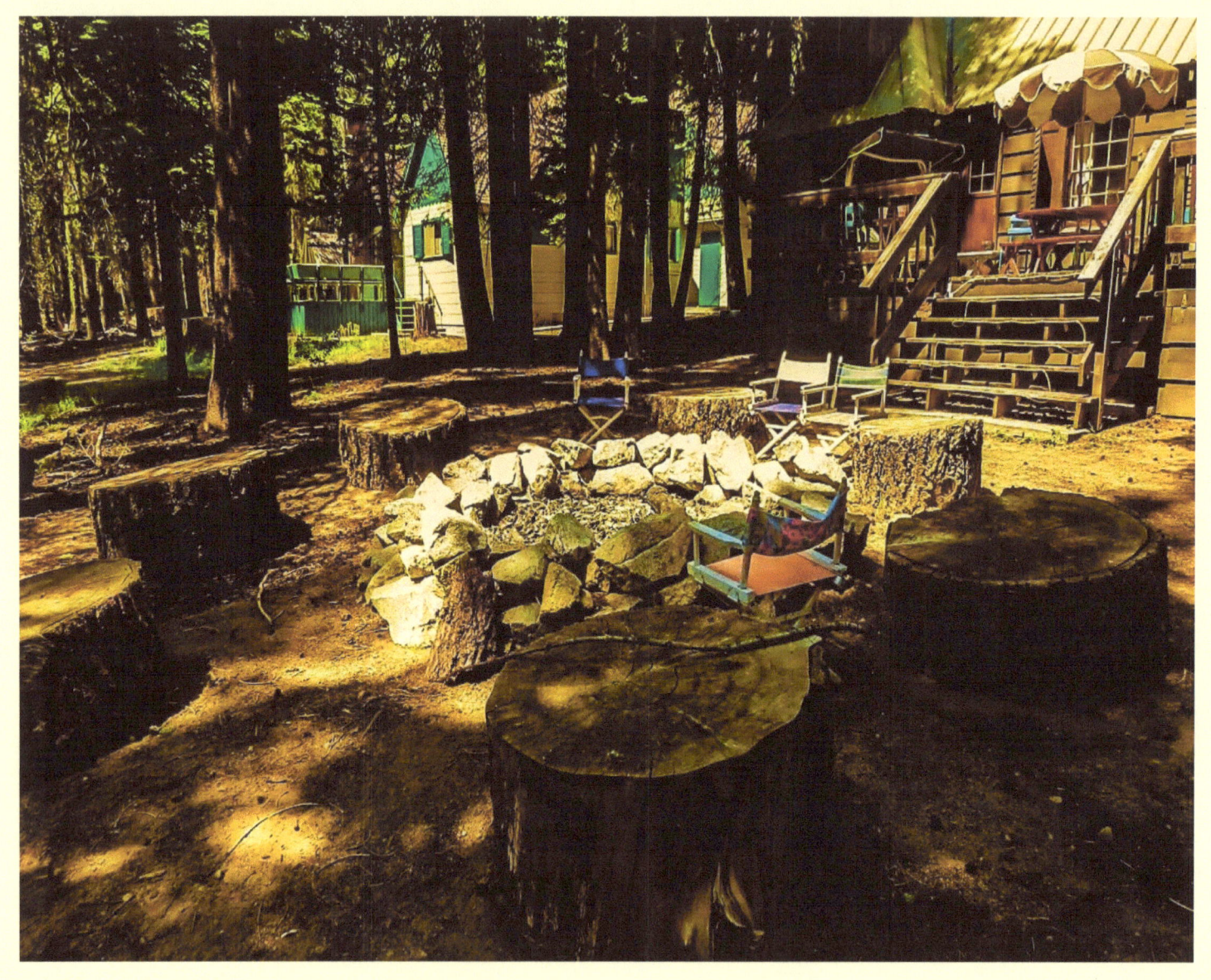

Finally arriving at that perfect cabin on that perfect lake –

*Where
the voyager
pauses
to embrace
wonderful
memories of
a blissful past –*

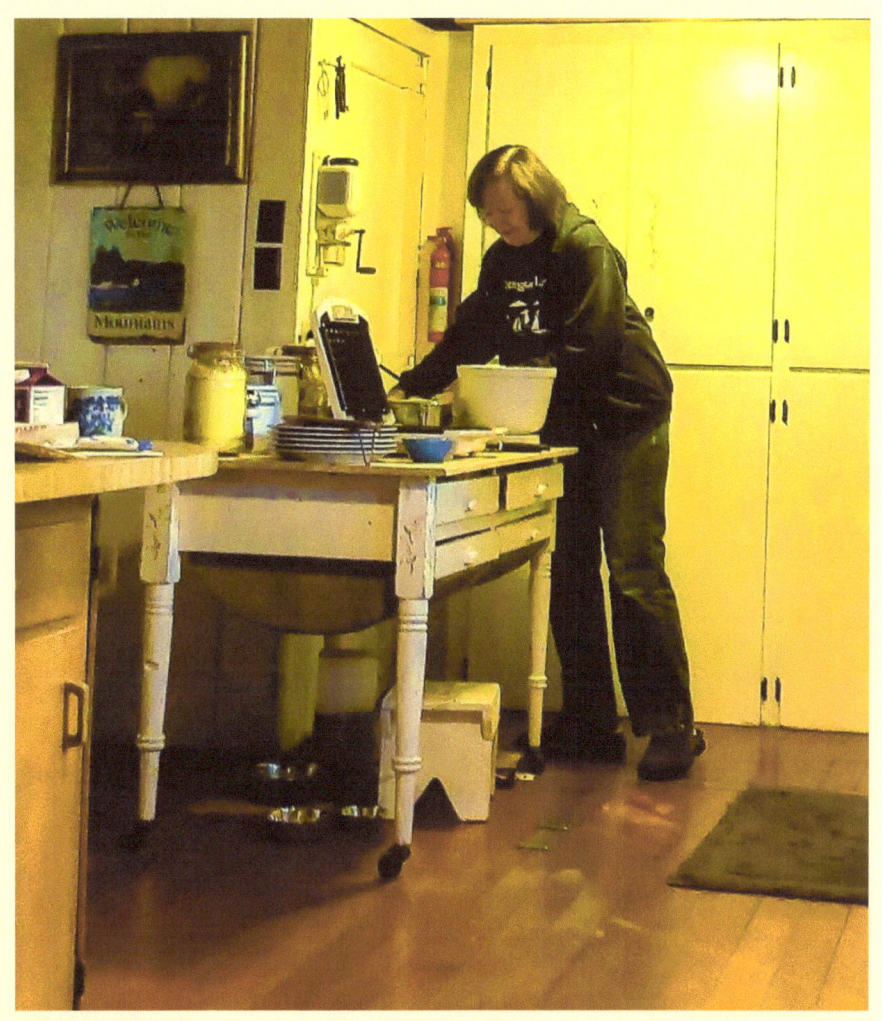

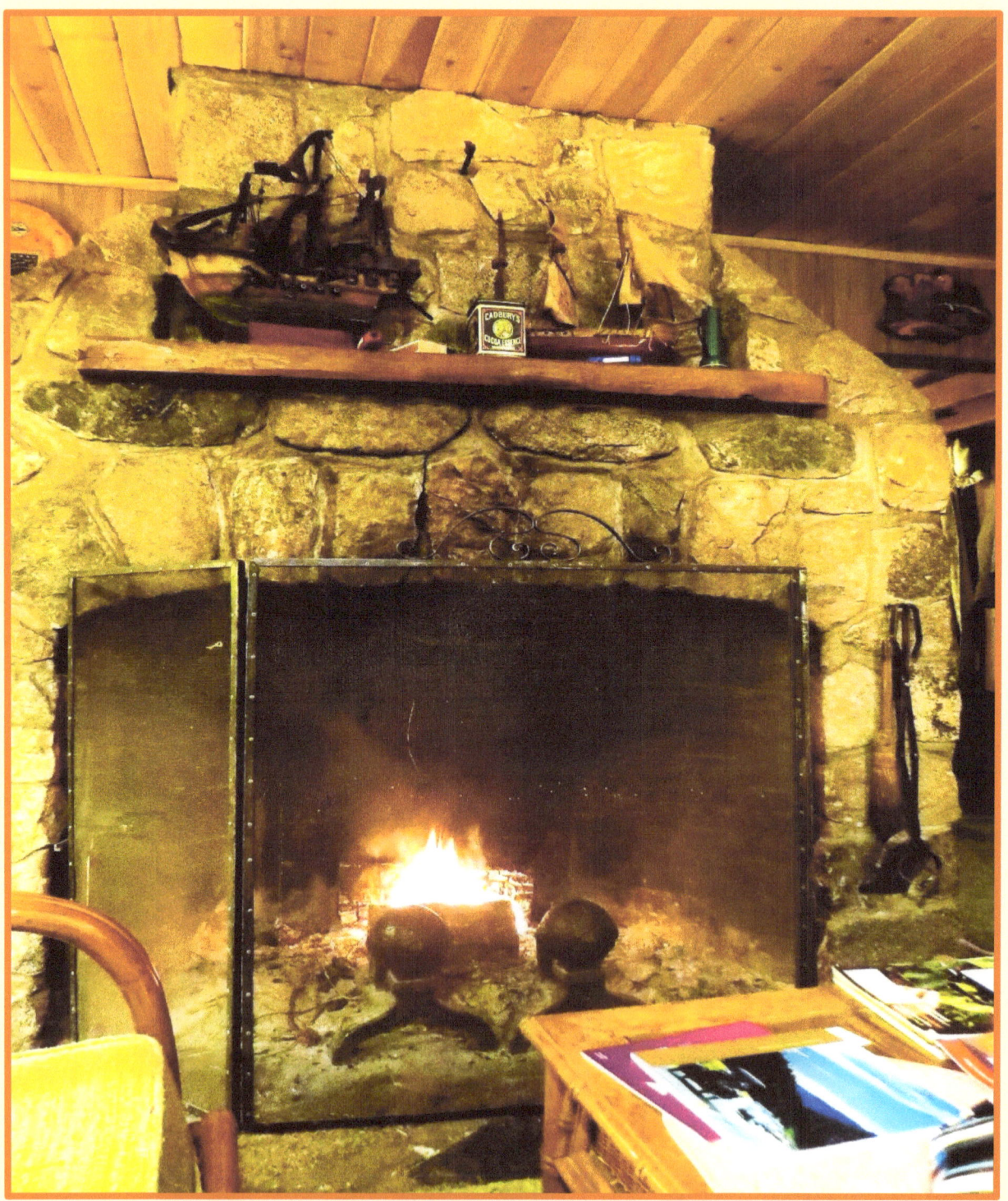

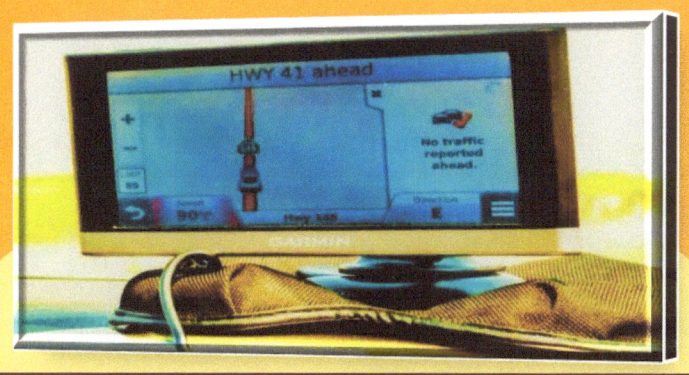

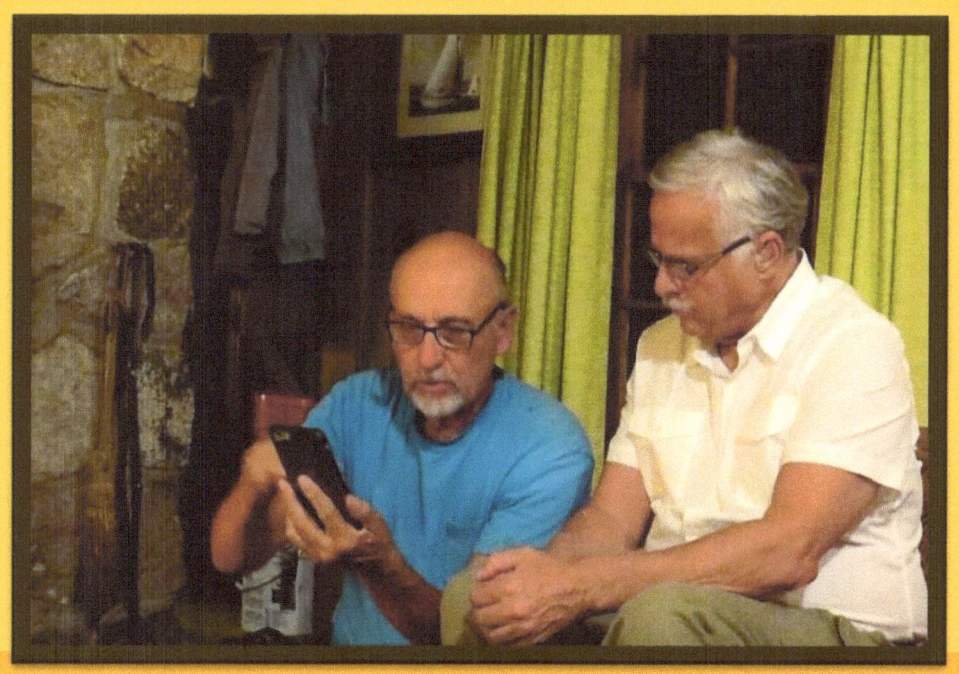

Then, destined to return to the present –

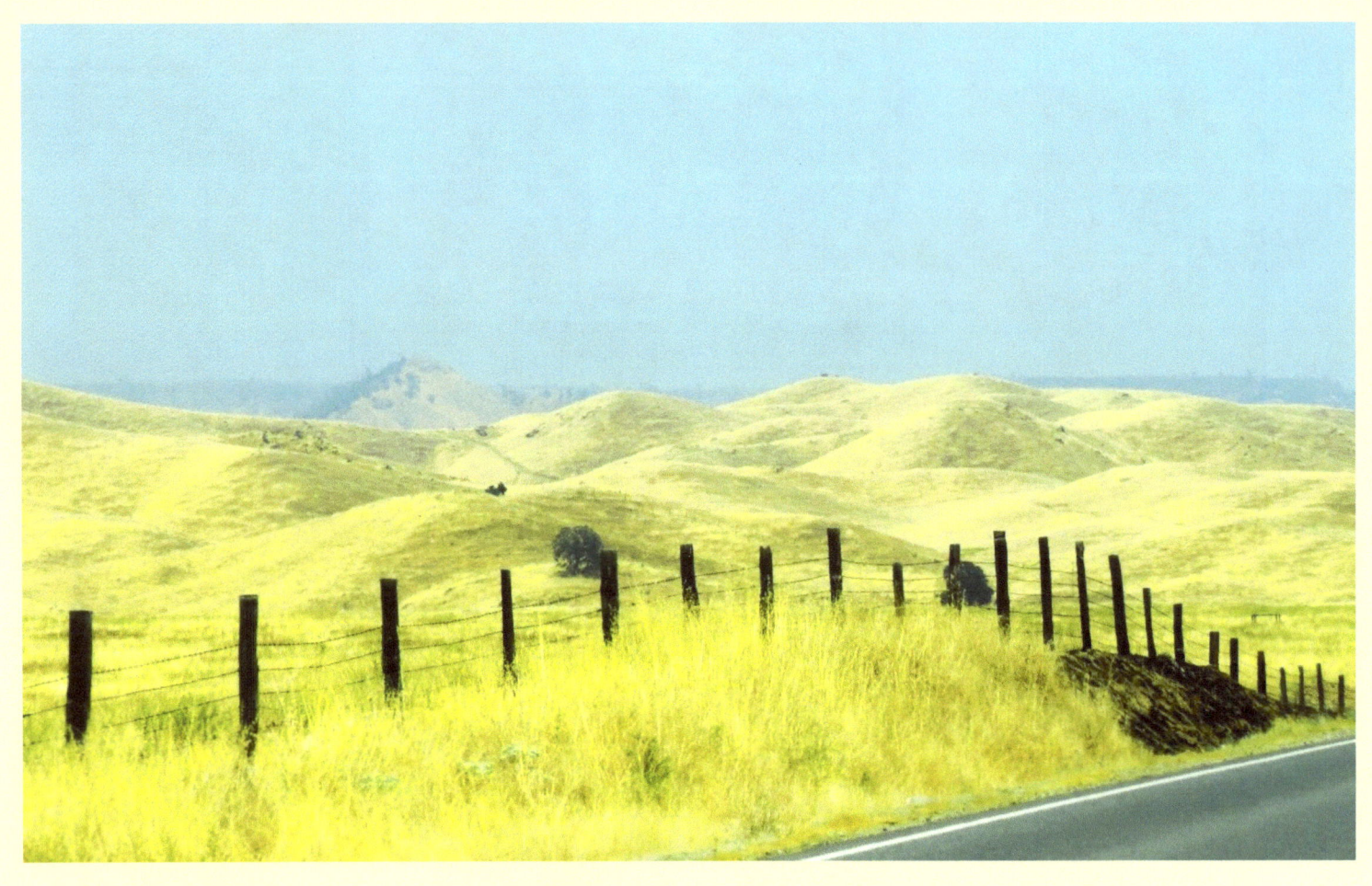

The pilgrim reluctantly asks for directions
Back to the 21st century,
Far away, somewhere to the east,
Beyond these desperately dry,
California golden hills –

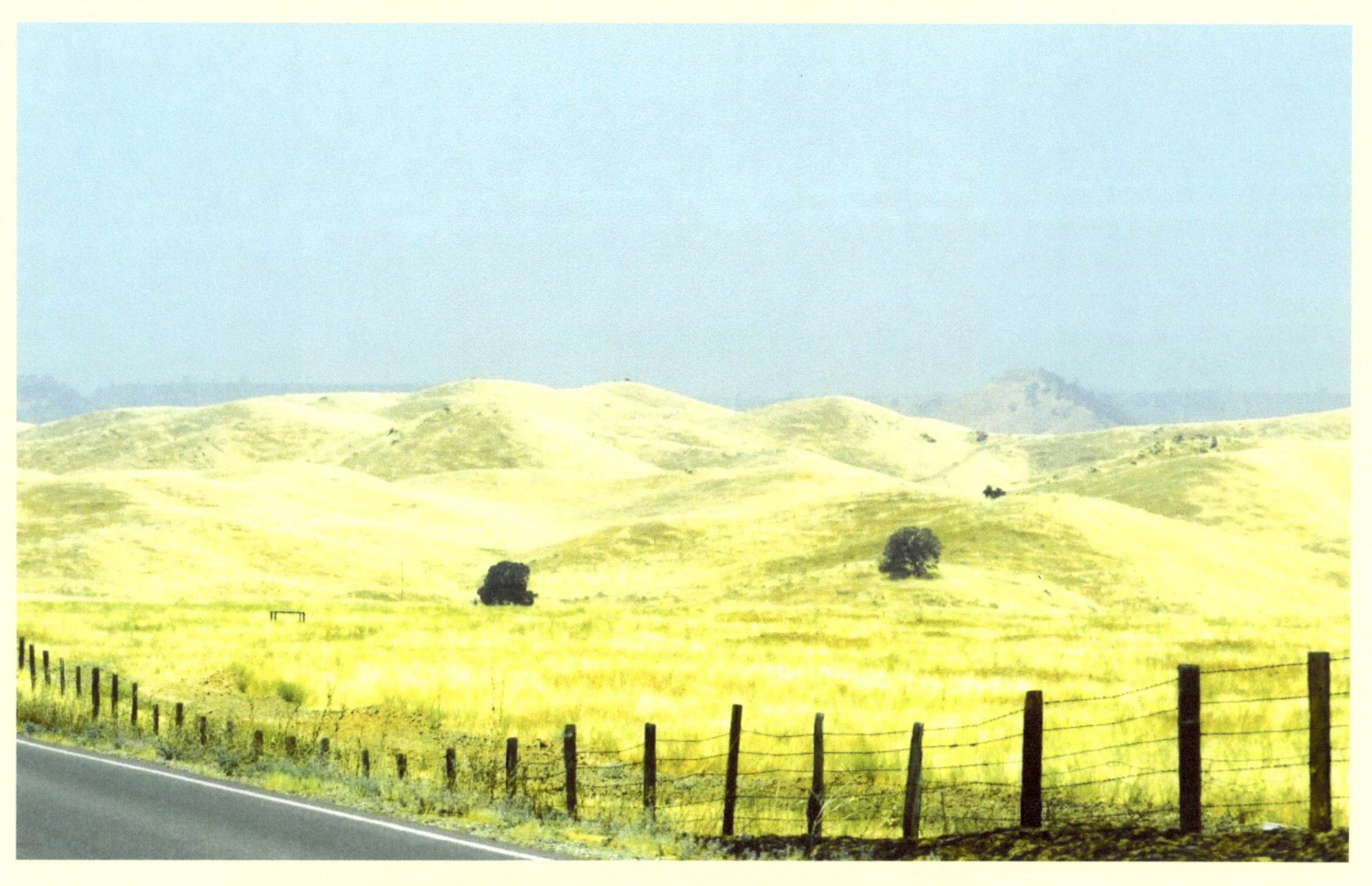

Across the high Sierras,
Through Nevada's captivating desert,
Up and over purple mountain majesties,
Down into the city,
And back into today …

We hope you have enjoyed perusing
this collection of Atwood's
Diversionary materials for areas of waiting

For a list of Cutting's other works,
Or to contact the artist,
Please go to www.atwoodcutting.com

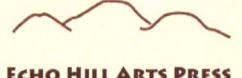

ECHO HILL ARTS PRESS

www.ingramcontent.com/pod-product-compliance
Lightning Source LLC
Chambersburg PA
CBHW050738180526
45159CB00003B/1275